RUDOLF STEINER

Rudolf Steiner

RUDOLF STEINER

aspects of his spiritual world-view

Anthroposophy

volume 3

Roy Wilkinson

TEMPLE LODGE
London

First published in 1980/1 as four booklets: *Journey through the Spheres*, *The Hosts of Heaven*, *The Cultivation of Thinking*, and *Christianity*

First published in current format in 1994 by Temple Lodge Publishing

A catalogue record for this book is available from the British Library

ISBN 0 904693 63 5

Cover by S. Gulbekian. Inset: Rudolf Steiner, 1916

Typeset by DP Photosetting, Aylesbury, Bucks
Printed and bound in Great Britain by Cromwell Press Limited, Broughton Gifford, Wiltshire

CONTENTS

NOTE

This book consists of the revised text of four booklets from a series of 12, first published in 1980/81 under the overall title Basic Anthroposophy. The word Anthroposophy was used by Rudolf Steiner to denote the particular world outlook, based on spiritual knowledge, which he represented. The booklets were intended as introductions to some of his basic concepts.

It should be noted that when the word 'man' or 'mankind' is used it is intended to represent human beings in general.

Roy Wilkinson
Forest Row
E. Sussex

1

LIFE BETWEEN DEATH AND REBIRTH

'Into Thy hands, O Lord . . .' These last words of Everyman in the famous medieval morality play testify to a trust in the Divinity and to a belief in life after death that is no longer quite so acceptable to the modern mind. In our scientific age faith is less in evidence and a spirit of enquiry has taken its place. Thus, among others, questions regarding destiny have assumed a greater importance than formerly and, among these, are matters appertaining to death and life hereafter. Attitudes to these matters are by no means uniform and in our mixed society it is only to be expected that we should find representatives of all shades of opinion.

There are, for instance, those who reject entirely the idea of a continued existence, believing that birth is a beginning and death an end. Possibly this view is due to fear, or to laziness in thinking, or to an unwillingness to face the consequences. Problems, however, do not disappear by being ignored.

Then there are those who admit the possibility of a continuation of life in some other form but take the attitude that they can wait until the time comes to cross the threshold, when all will be revealed.

This is a short-sighted view. If we are to undertake a journey, it is usual and reasonable to make some sort of preparation. If we are to travel into a strange land, it would seem advisable to gather such information as is available. If we are to sojourn in some particularly interesting place, it would be advantageous to learn about conditions there. In particular our stay would be much more fruitful if we had studied the country. If this is true of journeys in this world, then how much more significant must it be in the great adventure that awaits us beyond the grave.

There is a third category of human beings who accept the thought of a continuation of life as self-evident and search for such information as may be available.

Whether interested, apparently indifferent or openly agnostic, the human soul has certain needs and longs for assurances in matters of destiny, even if it does not consciously formulate questions. Such assurances *can* be found and much information *is* available.

Those who feel the urge to seek may find some of their requirements met by reference to history or literature since survival after death has been accepted as a fact since time immemorial. All the great religions testify to it and many of them to the idea of a rebirth of the human being on Earth, or what is termed reincarnation. Christianity does not proclaim this idea but at least it points to a spiritual world (Heaven) where human beings continue to exist and where they are united with friends and loved ones.

Philosophical thought, too, supports the idea. When Goethe, speaking of nature, says, 'Life is her fairest invention, death her means to create more life,' he is expressing nothing more than a fact of existence. Although the materialistic age produces a feeling of scepticism, it also stimulates the search for new ideas and many great minds of recent and modern times have expressed *belief* in a continued existence. (See vol. 1, chapter 2 of this work). There are, however, outstanding personalities who *know* and who can give knowledge from their own experience. Such individualities are endowed with exceptional powers. They possess the ability to penetrate the veil of physical existence and have direct access to the spiritual world. Rudolf Steiner had such a faculty. What he had to reveal is perfectly understandable and satisfying to an unprejudiced mind. But Rudolf Steiner goes beyond the mere answering of specific questions. He puts the answers in a world context showing how knowledge gained by the seeker is not only of significance for himself but for the whole Earth and evolution of mankind.

This chapter aims to give an outline of his indications with regard to human experience between death and rebirth. It presupposes familiarity with the idea of reincarnation.

The Continuity of Life

Life after death must be seen in the context of life before death but, since life does not begin at birth, we could also speak of life before birth. The child only comes physically naked into the world. Spiritually it brings gifts and qualities.

Let us consider for a moment a few general aspects of life, bearing in mind the title of this chapter.

In early infancy the child is entirely dependent on its surroundings and is naturally influenced by them. As it grows, what and how it learns form a foundation for its understanding and attitudes as a grown-up. The interest awakened in the child, the moral and religious background, will all influence the character of the adult. Skills, intellectual awareness, sociability, these are influenced by early training.

In day-to-day existence we do not start new projects every day but continue where we left off the day before. In the course of life different faculties develop and understanding matures. It is obvious that today's capabilities and capacities are dependent on yesterday's efforts and experiences, today's comprehension on yesterday's lessons. We may have forgotten the reading lesson but we have acquired the ability to read. We may have suffered some setback but it gives us an ability to sympathise with others. We may have exerted ourselves to learn a language; now we can understand and speak it.

Our daily life also brings us into contact with other people. There is our immediate family. We move in certain circles; we have co-workers; we may belong to a certain club, society or church. We realize that the world is peopled by all sorts and conditions of men. We meet new people and make new friends. We help others and are helped in turn. We also make acquaintance with unpleasant characters who radiate negative forces.

We ourselves have certain characteristics. We may be kind,

selfish, generous. We may be influenced by evil, succumb to temptation, be strong or weak-willed, independent or easily overruled. We may love and be loved; we may dislike our fellow humans and prefer isolation. Most of us have definite ideas, a particular way of thinking and a certain outlook on life. Some are very interested in what goes on around them, others less so.

Furthermore, in some way or other we are active in the world. We do something and our deeds have consequences. We do a kindness or the opposite; we do something creative or destructive. Everything has an effect. It is a sobering thought that in some measure, whatever we do, we leave our mark on the world. We might go so far as to say that everything we do, positive or negative, has an effect on the whole course of human evolution and should be judged in this light.

In the spiritual world there are corresponding factors and conditions.

As in early infancy the child learns things which last its whole life through and affect the life beyond, so after death (which is birth into the spiritual world) the individuality will learn things to last the whole of the period between death and rebirth and which will affect the new life on Earth.

As life here progresses in some logical sequence so does life there.

On Earth we enjoy sociability. We grow and develop in and by companionship. Here we are together with those who belong to us and the relationships continue. Here we meet people of dubious character, geniuses, men of high moral standing, and there, too, is variety. As we mutually influence one another here, so do we in the spiritual world.

When the human being dies, he casts off his material body and his eternal spiritual entity enters a spiritual world where his experiences and activities are a continuation of what went on before and where a new, wonderful and tremendously interesting phase of life begins.

After he has learned his lessons and reformed his nature, he is ready to embark on a new earthly existence.

Through the alternating experiences on Earth and in the spiritual world, that which lies at the centre of the human being—commonly referred to as the ego or spirit—is enriched. What has been experienced through existence in a physical body is developed in spiritland. There the spirit is refreshed, perhaps one could say recharged, with what is necessary for earthly life.

In considering the riddles of existence there comes a point when a question arises which cannot be answered—as yet. It concerns the goal of human existence.

It is difficult to visualize an ultimate goal and one is led to think that it must be beyond this evolution, beyond our comprehension and imagination at this stage. What can perhaps be said is that the fruits of all experience are incorporated in the ever-evolving human spirit on its path to become 'ideal' man. Greater revelation will come with greater capacity to understand.

One World

Man does not exist for himself alone. He is related in various ways to all the kingdoms of nature and to the universe itself. Everything is in some way related to everything else. In other words, we must think of the whole of the universe as a unity and man as a part of that unity, subject to the same laws. His continuous existence fits in with the whole idea of creation.

All nature works together and all parts of nature are interdependent. Throughout nature there are cycles of life and within the cycle death is a staging post. The plant grows, blossoms, forms seeds, dies, and a similar plant grows from the seed. Water is revitalized in the rain cycle; air is purified by vegetation; the torpor of winter is followed by the vitality of spring. Death and resurrection.

In nature there is order but it exists not only in nature. It is inbuilt in the universe. By day we observe the regular passage of the Sun across the heavens, by night the procession of stars and planets. We note the established rhythm of day and night.

Man is a part of nature and a part of the cosmos. He is one with nature and one with the cosmos although he has a certain independence. He takes part in the rhythms of nature and of the cosmos. In fact cosmic rhythms are reflected in his own. Actual numbers demonstrate the relationship between the Sun's movement and man's breathing and life-span, but the great rhythm of life is that of expansion and contraction. The plant grows on this principle. Day and night, summer and winter illustrate it. It is reflected in man's alternation of waking and sleeping, or, in a wider context, of birth and death. In the state of wakefulness there is continual wear taking place, evidenced by the feeling of tiredness. In sleep there is a restoring process although man is not conscious of this. During sleep the spiritual part of man has sojourned in its own home, the spiritual world, and it has brought back fresh forces for physical existence. Activity between death and rebirth is similar, but it is directed not to restoring the present body but to building up a new one from the forces of the universe.

Man, Earth, nature, cosmos, spiritual beings are all parts of a unity, parts of a spirit-filled, self-sustaining universe. Life and movement are in continuous harmony. There are no sudden endings. Life persists.

We are inclined to think of the spiritual world, if indeed we think of it at all, as something remote, separate and different. Different it is but neither remote nor separate, for physical world and spiritual world are really one.

A simple example will illustrate the point. A plant needs soil, light, air, warmth for its growth but there is a strange power inherent in the plant which gives it the possibility to grow, and to grow into its own particular form. This has nothing to do with physical forces. It is something non-perceptible to ordinary vision and might be termed—in a general sense—spiritual. Thus the plant is a manifestation of a spiritual force and since this force must exist somewhere we can say that it is centred in the spiritual world.

The plant dies and its spiritual force is dissipated, but that is not to say that it is lost. New plants grow, imbued with the same force and hence we could look upon the spiritual as having an enduring quality.

We can look upon the human being in a similar way. On the one hand he has a physical body and, on the other, something less tangible to which we refer—again in a general sense—as the spirit. Normally we consider that the spirit dwells within the body during earthly existence but that its home is in another realm into which it is released at death.

It is interesting to note that in the process of ageing the body changes its substance every seven years so that the adult cannot be the same as the child. Yet the personality remains. Obviously there is something present of lasting character, something which we also term the spirit.

Following the same line of thought we can consider the whole of creation in the same light. In fact we have good authority for it. The Bible tells us that God created Heaven and the Earth, and man in His own image.

Thus the heavenly bodies which appear to us as physical orbs also have a spiritual background. They, too, are manifestations of the spiritual, in this case of higher beings. They represent the spheres through which the human spirit travels.

Nevertheless, our modern minds think in terms of two worlds. Usually we are aware of the physical only but, if the faculty of perception were sufficiently developed, we could be aware of the spiritual world while still living in the flesh. Death would then become a minor experience. In present circumstances death marks the end of one sort of consciousness and the beginning of another.

Earthly Deeds and Attitudes: Their Consequences

It is not intended to give full explanations here but only significant indications.

As mortals we have strengths and weaknesses of character and what we have made of ourselves is reflected in the spiritual world.

Let us consider the case of a person who has lived an immoral, dissolute life on Earth. In the spiritual world such a person will not be in a position to partake fully of the life there. His experiences will be limited. He will have only a dim, twilight consciousness and will not be able to attract to himself the whole of the normally required forces for a new incarnation. Hence when he next appears on the physical plane he will have a weakness of some sort. On the other hand, a morally disposed person will have greater contacts with the helping higher beings, the Hierarchies, and will attract the right assistance for future health and balance.

Or take the case of an out-and-out materialist, one who on Earth has rejected all knowledge of spiritual matters. In his new surroundings he will be like one lost in the wilderness without chart or compass. By contrast, one who has busied himself on Earth with ideas of a spiritual nature will be better orientated and will achieve greater harmony in his next life on Earth.

It is a fact of life that not all people live to a ripe old age. Parting is always a matter of sorrow, and when a young person dies the feeling of loss is all the greater. Though suffering may be caused, it may be a consoling thought that dying young has another aspect. There is a compensating effect in that the person concerned will achieve a strong position in a future life, or that he will be endowed with a strong will, a strong character or strength to fulfil a special mission. The fact of leaving the Earth in early years also has an effect in the spiritual world. Here such individuals are 'idealists', bringing to the dead the unfinished impulses from their lives and showing that there is something spiritual on the Earth. They act as a counter to materialism. Dying young also releases forces that can be used by the higher beings to help souls who are faltering in their progress.

By contrast, the result of living to an old age results in greater inner activity in the next incarnation and a less defined vocation.

Those who have failed to meet life's difficulties and have taken their own lives face particular problems. For them not only are the normal desires appertaining to the body still present, without the means of gratification, but the sudden and violent separation from the body is felt as a greater deprivation than if death had taken place naturally.

(It might be mentioned here that those in difficulty in the beyond can be helped by those still on Earth. See volume 2, chapter 2 of this series.)

Those human beings who have worked on Earth with enthusiasm and devotion, and not merely out of a sense of duty, are in an advantageous position. They can become co-workers and helpers of the higher powers, receiving advancement through the fact of close association. This also applies to those who learn to adapt themselves properly to their environment, that is to say, those who cope with life, however it presents itself. Since a man is on Earth not only to gather for himself the fruits of experience but also to bring impulses into the spiritual world, such beings are strengthened by positive attitudes and in turn they can radiate health-giving forces to the Earth.

It might be said that many people on Earth find themselves in dull routine work where enthusiasm and devotion are difficult to generate. This objection is perfectly valid but it is equally valid that man possesses an inner moral strength and if he can develop this sufficiently he can carry out whatever tasks life imposes. If his work does not inspire enthusiasm, then he can take the opportunity to be creative in some other field.

Moreover the Hierarchies have gifts to bestow on those who are worthy to receive them. Negative attitudes on Earth, no thoughts on the supersensible, result in no awareness of what the spiritual world can offer. It means a lack of some good quality in a future life.

This is particularly the case with those who, rejecting all ideas of a spiritual nature, devote their energies to making for themselves a material paradise of ease and comfort.

A lack of conscience on Earth can also result in a human being coming under the influence of evil spirits in the spiritual world—again with repercussions in a future life.

There is, however, another aspect of these matters which goes beyond the personal. As on Earth we affect our environment so do we in the beyond, although it must be appreciated that environment there is a vastly different matter. It is also possible to take harmful impulses into the spiritual world and these also affect the Hierarchies. These lofty beings are the spiritual background of the terrestrial kingdoms of nature and they are influenced by their association with man. Evil thoughts, evil feelings bring about changes in their character, and, as they change, so do conditions on Earth. This means that man is ultimately responsible for such things as earthquakes and volcanic eruptions, even the destruction of continents. As an example one might recall the destruction of Atlantis through the wickedness of men (Noah and the story of the Flood). Evolution is bound up with changes in the Earth.

In spite of appearances we inhabit an orderly world in which there must be balance. Balance is achieved by compensating. In biblical terms it is reaping as one sows. Should we meet difficulties in this life or the next, we should not complain since they are probably of our own making. We may even bring illnesses on ourselves through our failures.

This law of compensation, in particular the idea of carrying over debts or credits into another incarnation, is what is usually understood by the oriental word 'karma'. In older times, a man knew that if he suffered some inability on Earth it was because he had not acquired the right forces on his previous journey through the spheres, and he would resolve to make good the next time round. The physicians, too, who were initiates, could offer guidance.

The Nature of the Spiritual World and the Path through the Spheres

Dr Steiner continually points out the difficulties of explaining, in earthly language, matters appertaining to the spirit. What is said can only be taken as an approximation or as an equivalent. It is necessary to try to form new concepts. In fact even when one uses the expression 'spiritual world' there is something of a contradiction. 'World' infers something solid. Instead of spiritual world one might equally say a state of mind.

Using the language of approximation we can say that at death the human being enters an environment where he no longer perceives the solid objects of the physical world. Instead of stones, plants, animals, stars, he is aware of spiritual beings which are the counterpart of physical existence. Even his own thoughts and those of friends left behind manifest as beings. Time and space do not exist.

We have to try to form a different idea of the being of man and of his relationships with fellow humans. On Earth we are bounded by our skin and separated physically. In the spiritual world there is an intermingling and an interpenetration. Relationships are a matter of consciousness. In a crude sort of way we might think of souls occupying the same place but they are unaware of one another unless the requisite consciousness has been developed. This is enkindled by inward feeling. The ability to perceive has to come from within. Only individuals already acquainted with one another can perceive each other in the spiritual world. Acquaintance can only be acquired on Earth.

There are also higher beings present but no human being is conscious of them unless he has acquired the necessary inner powers. The greater his effort to obtain knowledge of spiritual realities while still on Earth, the greater his consciousness between death and rebirth.

A different experience from that on Earth is for man to feel himself united with the cosmos. At one stage of his progress he feels that the planetary and other heavenly forces are not only outside but also within him, just as, on Earth, he feels that the organs of the heart, lungs, etc, are within him. He feels as if he is spread over the cosmos and looks, so to speak, from the circumference to the centre. It is as if he is duplicated, gathering forces from the different points of the heavens to form his being. A person on Earth with the necessary spiritual development would feel, like the rest of us, that his heart and other organs were within him, but he would also feel that the planetary forces are within these since the body is built up from the forces of the cosmos.

In this connection it is interesting to note that the alchemists of old referred to bodily organs by the names of the planets.

Theology speaks of Heaven and Hell, evoking the concept of regions. The one is a place of eternal bliss and the other of eternal torment. Both must be extremely boring.

Nevertheless the ideas have some justification except that it is more reasonable to think of a series of regions, some of which may be pleasant and some unpleasant, but where there is continual activity as the human being passes through them.

Although one speaks of regions in this context, they must not be thought of as spatially side by side since, in the spiritual sense, they interpenetrate one another. Regions in our case can be equated with spheres but these spheres are not the physical orbs we see in the heavens. They are their spiritual environment, the homes of the Hierarchies.

To speak of a journey is also not quite correct and such an expression in this context must be understood figuratively or imaginatively.

The experience between between death and rebirth is a 'journey' of the human spirit through the planetary spheres to the realm of the fixed stars and back again. As an approximate outline description, we could think that on the outward path we experience the events of our past life, all that we have done on Earth. Now detached from the body we relive them almost as memories but these memories are real, inner experiences. On Earth we know only rudiments of such as, for instance, when pangs of conscience trouble us, or when we rejoice over a good deed.

We meet and accept the judgement of our actions and learn eagerly how they must be compensated. We cannot make amends at this stage. Knowledge and insight will be obtained but only on Earth can things be rectified. What is acquired is a guiding light for a new incarnation.

On our journey we inscribe, as it were, a spiritual record in the planetary spheres. We meet those with whom we have been connected on Earth and also heavenly beings who help us on our way. We reach the highest sphere and turn again towards the Earth, collecting what is our own, the results of our former deeds.

These are woven into the pattern of our future life so that we shall be led subconsciously to situations where we can make good past errors or receive due rewards for work well done. According to what has been deposited on the way up and the measure of sympathy with which we have passed through each sphere, so will forces be given to us by higher beings. They

will help in transforming what was learnt on Earth into ability
for the next incarnation. With their help we build the prototype of a body to accord with our nature and needs. We must
choose the right time to be born, the right place and the right
parents, guided by the Hierarchies. All this must be arranged
from the spiritual world even to the extent of influencing the
coming together of our ancestors many years in advance. The
human being is certainly active in all this but not indepen-
dently active as on Earth, where individual independence is
conditioned by bodily existence. Yet we are not passive.
Between death and rebirth we co-operate with the higher
beings.

The First Experience after Death: The Panorama of the Past Life

In volume 1, chapter 1 of this series the human being was
described in a fourfold aspect: physical body, etheric, astral
and ego. The physical body consists of material substance, the
other three are non-material. A comparison has already been
made between sleep and death. Now the processes involved
can be explained in greater detail.

In ordinary waking life all four principles are closely connected. A certain separation takes place in sleep. The life
forces are still active in the physical body and we can therefore
deduce that the physical and etheric remain united. But in
sleep we have no conscious feeling and no consciousness of
ourselves and thus we can assume that the vehicles of these are
absent. In other words the astral and ego have detached
themselves. At death not only the astral and ego but also the
etheric leaves the physical body.

Sleep	Physical body, Etheric	Astral, Ego
Death	Physical body	Etheric, Astral, Ego

The physical body, now subject only to physical laws, disintegrates. The etheric dissolves into the world-ether from

which it was originally formed. The other members progress into other realms, but before describing their path something must be said concerning the separation of the physical and etheric bodies.

If we say that this takes approximately three days, it must be understood that this only applies to earthly reckoning. The individuality concerned has no concept of time but during this period he has a wonderful experience. His whole past life is spread out before him as a vast panorama. It is an experience that is not entirely unknown even in this world. There are records of people who have been on the brink of death by drowning or falling who have seen such a picture but who have lived to tell the tale.

The vision fades as the etheric body dissolves but an after-effect of it is preserved. His constitution is now twofold, soul and spirit.

The Region of Purification (Purgatory, Kamaloka)

In order to understand what is next experienced, we must again consider man's nature. On Earth the human being has many desires and passions which belong to the sense world and which can only be gratified through the physical body. He also has subconscious longings. These feelings belong to the soul and they do not immediately disperse at death. They continue to be felt but now there is no body through which satisfaction can be obtained. The pure spirit in man cannot advance further while connected with and hampered by a soul with bodily desires. The urges must therefore be purged. They cannot now be satisfied and they are experienced as a burning thirst or a consuming fire. This is the explanation of what is usually called purgatory or, in Eastern terminology, Kama-loka. The soul has to learn not to long for those things which can only be satisfied through the body, and through such non-gratification the desires are extinguished. If this appears to be a torment, then it must be remembered that it is a torment which is desired by the human being concerned in order that further progress may be made. It is a process of purification.

In a similar way, thoughts, wishes, remembrances dependent on physical existence must be cast off.

It is obvious that the intensity of experience here will depend on the character of the person. Those with the most earthly desires will have the most to purify.

But this is not the only thing the human being has to endure in this region. Again a little diversion must be made in order that matters may be clear. We must consider what happens during sleep.

In normal day-to-day existence the human being alternates between sleeping and waking. In sleep he is normally unconscious of what is going on around him but this does not mean that he is inactive. It is true that the body rests in bed but the spiritual part of his being leaves it and soars into another realm where the events of the day are recollected. All that a man has done, felt or thought is reviewed and the angelic hosts who dwell in this world pass judgement on events.

After death the human being relives, so-to-speak, his sleep life and he does this in reverse order. He first experiences events immediately preceding his death and goes back to the moment of birth. It is a life of memories but of memories which evoke a reaction, for now he feels the pain, the suffering, joy, etc., which he caused others. In these recapitulations, therefore, he is at the receiving end of his own deeds. What he gave, he now receives. Any distress he has caused others, including the animal world, he will now experience himself. It is a salutary reversal but at this stage nothing can be done by way of compensation. Nevertheless, insight is given. Man realizes that every one of his acts has consequences. He realizes the significance of his deeds for the whole of the rest of the world. An impulse is given to make good where necessary, but this, however, can only be done on Earth in a future incarnation. Thus man begins to form ideas of future destiny.

There is a meeting together here of those who were connected with one another in life and the significance of common destiny begins to unfold. In meeting, however, another sort of lesson is learned. The human being has no way of disguising his moral nature. Whereas on Earth the physical appearance of a man may tell nothing of his moral character, in this region, in his spiritual appearance, this is exposed and cannot be cast off. He is thus recognized by others for what he is and, in turn, he recognizes others. What on Earth was hidden, perhaps in the deep recesses of conscience, now becomes manifest. His own feelings of aversion or affection call forth a reaction in the other person so that he sees himself reflected in others as if in a mirror.

These things are also an objective judgement and give further impulse to correction, improvement or compensation. Another point to note is that perception, and hence progress, depend on a willingness to see. The individual has to become conscious of others in this spiritual world by means of his own individual effort.

Besides fellow humans, there are other beings in this region. On the one hand there are evil creations who derive nourishment from man's passions. The excarnated human being is faced with horrible forms which instil fear into him but in actual fact they are manifestations of his own lower urges. On the other hand, there are also higher beings and man is conscious of their joy or sorrow at what he brings with him from earthly life. This is felt as a judgement. Forces of sympathy or antipathy stream from them according to what is brought and these provide guidance.

As here on Earth there are some people who find life easy and some otherwise, so also in the spiritual world there are those who have a relatively easy passage and others who meet difficulties. There is, however, one great difference. In physical life it is quite possible that the honest and the just may suffer hardships and the rogues and villains have a life of ease and comfort. But the manner of life after death is determined by justice. There is compensation but it must not be thought that justice is something imposed by an outside agency. It is something sought by the individual for it is his means of progress.

With regard to the time-aspect, time can only be reckoned in relation to the Earth but, since we reckon time between incarnations, we can think of periods spent in various regions. In this respect and in earthly terms, the sojourn in this region of purification lasts for about a third of the lifetime, i.e. the same period as has been spent asleep. Those who have lived for a long time are likely to have more to shed than those who die early, while anyone who dies very young would have attracted few burdens and passes through quickly.

The Period of 'Education'

At the end of the Kamaloka period, i.e. when the grossest physical urges have been overcome, the spirit is able to cast off an astral substance, an astral corpse, which falls away like the physical body at death.

Now the human being traverses various soul regions in each of which he has some specific experience. He is 'educated' by beings of a higher order. It is almost like progressing through different classes in school and being taught by different teachers. But his capacity to understand and to receive benefit is conditioned throughout by his previous attitude on Earth. A mind which was orientated towards the spirit will have provided a better basis for understanding than that of a materialist. Earlier feelings of love and sympathy also play a part as well as morality and religious conviction.

Up to now his experience has been one of beholding, of vision, but now he comes into a region where he is made more conscious of the far-reaching consequences of his deeds and how they may influence the future. Angelic beings remind him of his actions on Earth and that he has to reckon with these. He becomes more aware of wrongs committed against others but at this stage he can still do nothing to compensate. It is a further painful experience.

In Kamaloka the human being knew only the reactions of the spiritual beings who showed pleasure or displeasure at what was brought to them. Now he is permeated by their forces which give him a sort of moral consciousness or what one might call a cosmic conscience.

The conditions under which he lives in this region are dependent on morality in the previous Earth existence. A moral person enjoys sociability with others and with higher beings. This, of course, means advancement, but an immoral person lives in isolation, excluded from the community, and leads a restricted and solitary existence. This is felt as a torment for the individual but it also has a negative effect on the world generally.

In the next region the 'teachers' add description and explanation of the former earthly existence. What is decisive for man's understanding of these matters and for his social life is his former religious disposition ('religious' is to be understood in the broadest sense as having some understanding that the physical is transitory, that a spiritual essence permeates the physical, that man is of divine creation and immortal, whatever the creed). Human contacts here are like with like. For example, Hindus will find fellow-Hindus; Christians, fellow-Christians.

In his upward progress man continues to receive instruction from the higher beings at a higher level. He acquires a great knowledge of destiny. He learns more about his relationships with other humans and how these will affect the future. But more than this, he is now expanding so far into the cosmos that he begins to feel at one with it. Whereas in physical life he had felt Earth to be his home, he now feels that he is a creature born out of the spiritual world. He comprehends more of the spiritual realms and their connection with the Earth. He becomes aware of the interworking of the planetary spheres and this awareness becomes auditory. He 'hears' what the old Pythagoreans used to call the 'Music of the Spheres'.

The conditions for full participation and receipt of benefits here are a previous appreciation on Earth for all religions, including what was Christlike in another person even if his faith was not Christianity.

Fulfilment and Transformation

But now it is not only a question of education. Together with the Hierarchies the individuality begins to work on the spiritual pattern of his new physical body. This has a certain relationship with the old one. The previous physical body will be transformed—spiritually speaking—into the prototype of the new head. With a little imagination it is not difficult to observe a threefoldness in the head which corresponds to the whole physical organism. The dome is the head part, cheek bones are like arms and the lower jaw, legs. There are also corresponding functions. Sense impressions belong to the head; nose and lungs are related, and so are the jaws and digestion.

The way is taken into still loftier spiritual realms. As in previous regions, consciousness depends on the attention the individual has given to spiritual values while on Earth. If sufficiently awake, he now finds himself in a world of pure spirit and feels himself as a spirit among spirits. He realizes that thoughts are living realities and that in this world they are beings. He appreciates how the spiritual permeates everything physical and he recognizes the spiritual background of all material things.

If he is sufficiently advanced he has a remembrance of earlier lives and a preview of future ones. He has a survey of all his human connections. Earthly life is seen from a cosmic viewpoint. He recognizes what has been of spiritual value. He has reached the furthest limit of his journey and the point of return.

He comes into closer relationship with mighty divine creative beings who guide, help and influence his future to be in harmony with what is true and spiritual. It is a sublime experience to be among the Hierarchies.

Consciously or unconsciously the human being works with the higher powers, continuing the task already started, transforming the spiritual substance he has brought with him into capacities. The spiritual pattern of the body needs more shaping. Account must be taken of deserts and merits and whatever is required to fulfil the new destiny. This body is built from the ingredients of the whole spiritual universe, by forces streaming in from the cosmos. As a magnet takes its direction from forces outside itself so does the body take shape under the influence of outside forces that are spiritual. Its final appearance on Earth is a manifestation of this spirituality but the finished form must fit the individuality. Time and place of birth as well as ancestry must be determined in accordance with karmic needs.

The forces of the cosmic powers now stream into man, giving him the feeling that they are more and more active within him. He is inspired to work towards their goal of ideal man. He experiences himself far more intensively as an individual, and as this feeling grows richer the vision of the spiritual environment begins to fade. A longing for the physical world develops.

Descent to a New Incarnation

In the outer spheres the spiritual pattern of the new body has been formed in accordance with the individuality's new requirements. Experiences have been changed into capacities, the spirit enriched.

During the upward journey a record of perfections and imperfections has been left in the various regions. Now on the journey to Earth again these records, or rather the compensating aspects, become part of a person's karma, that is, the pattern of life. They are woven into his being.

As the individuality descends into the soul world, he gathers substance or forces from the astral world to form his own astral body. This will contain directives in accordance with former deeds, directives that will influence his future.

The spiritual Hierarchies take part in the weaving of the path of destiny.

Coming into lower regions there is now a feeling of separation and a loss of consciousness of the upper realms. The individual seeks the right basis for a new incarnation.

From the world ether the individuality gathers etheric forces for his new body. The strength or otherwise of these is also determined by previous deeds and character.

There is a right time and a right place to be born to accord with requirements. Birth takes place in both an earthly and a cosmic setting. The personal constellation is a moral inheritance.

The parents provide the physical basis for life on Earth. As the individuality descends and connects himself more closely with her who is to be his mother, he has the longing to be on Earth to fulfil his karma. Immediately before incarnation he has a preview of earthly life in general outline. During the embryo period his consciousness is dimmed to dream consciousness with which he lives at the beginning of earthly existence.

2

THE SPIRITUAL HIERARCHIES

In ordinary everyday life we live in a world that provides us with a constant stream of impressions. There are innumerable physical objects around us of which we are dimly aware but of which we can suddenly become conscious if the occasion arises. For instance, we are much more aware of the car that nearly runs us down, the kerb stone that is out of alignment, the dog that snarls or wags its tail when we approach it, or the fact that so many people exist when we are trying to get through a crowd. The physical world is made very obvious to us in all the solid objects we encounter. But there are physical objects that have less solidity, as, for instance, water and air. Like solids, our awareness of water can easily be heightened— we need only fall into the river. The volatile air is a little more remote and our consciousness of it is perhaps increased when it is polluted or rarified as in a stuffy atmosphere or up a high mountain. Light and warmth are also more noticeable in their absence or abundance.

Thus a multitude of impressions from the natural world reaches us through our senses and affects us. But we are, in addition, subject to more subtle influences of which we are less aware. On a sunny day people are inclined to feel more cheerful than on a wet one. The geological structure of the environment, too, has an effect on health.

There is also the matter of human relationships. The people with whom we come in contact influence us and we, in turn, influence them, not necessarily consciously.

We can proceed further into a less definable world. Ideas and inspirations come into our minds. We are sometimes led to actions which we would not normally perform. It is not

unknown for some tragedy to be averted through a sudden
and apparently inexplicable intervention. In such a case sen-
sitive souls speak of a guiding power or a Guardian Angel.

There are people who perceive beings in nature, in the earth,
in the water, in the flowers and the trees. These nature spirits
or elementals are known by other names, such as gnomes,
undines, sylphs and salamanders. They are the 'little folk' of
the Irish. Of people with such a faculty we say they are a little
'fey', i.e. they have some primitive form of spiritual vision.

Bearing these matters in mind we can say that our normal
consciousness of the world is partial. It can, of course, be
developed, not only with respect to the material world but also
beyond the immediate world of sense perception.

We can extend our survey. Even a cursory consideration of
the natural or the human world will show that both are full of
infinite wisdom. The way a plant grows, receives its nourishment, absorbs light, warmth and air, produces flower and
seed, can be a never-ending source of wonder. The instinct that
guides a bird to build its nest and care for its young is nothing
short of miraculous. The human form is an astounding work
of art and skill. Looking into the heavens we note that the
movements of Sun, Moon and stars are obviously regulated.
We can agree with Hamlet: 'There are more things in heaven
and earth, Horatio, than are dreamt of in your philosophy'.

Wonder is the gate of knowledge. A deeper contemplation
of nature can reveal some of its secrets. It may call forth some
response in the human soul which is akin to a religious feeling.
The question may arise as to what is expressed in objects and
events since these are not always immediately explicable on
their own ground. We may rightly ask after an agency which
reveals itself in the phenomena, and, if there is such an agency,
what its nature is.

Historically, except in relatively modern times, there has
always been an answer. This was God or the gods. If we look
back in history for a moment, we note that the ancient peoples
had quite different faculties from modern man. They were
familiar with 'gods'. Their minds were more attuned to a
spiritual world and less to a physical and they were aware that
in the spiritual world there lived higher beings.

All primitive peoples and all past civilizations have had their gods. The Hindus had a numerous array. The ancient Egyptians recognized that at one time higher beings had led them but withdrawn in favour of human or semi-human leaders. The Greeks and, to a lesser extent the Romans, looked up to their especial divinities. The Norsemen, the Celts and the Anglo-Saxons had theirs.

The names of the gods or divinities are as varied as the peoples and it is not proposed to list them here. But they also appear in the Christian tradition and certain of them are mentioned by name in the Bible. References to Angels are numerous. Isaiah had a vision of the Seraphim. It is the Cherubim who are set to guard the Garden of Eden. Jude refers to the Archangel Michael; St Paul speaks of Thrones, Dominions, Principalities and Powers.

In the western world the gods have receded, that is to say, with the development of thinking and its preoccupation with the material world the spiritual vision of earlier ages has been lost. (See vol. 1, chapter 3 of this work). This does not necessarily mean, however, that the gods no longer exist and for those who, like Rudolf Steiner, possess extended faculties of consciousness, the world of higher beings is still accessible. If we can consider the material world as an expression of the physical, then a greater understanding is achieved when the role of these beings is understood. Not only are we surrounded and influenced on all sides by physical events and objects but we are also continually surrounded and influenced by spiritual happenings and beings.

The title of this chapter contains the word Hierarchies. In its usual worldly sense 'hierarchy' is understood as a grade or rank in priestly government. In its derivation the word means 'sacred rulership'. In the present context, Hierarchies refers to the ranks of higher or angelic beings.

Here on Earth man lives in the physical world with the three lower kingdoms of nature: the animal, plant and mineral. Above him, in the spiritual world, are three ranks of higher beings, reaching to the Godhead which is so far beyond him as to be incomprehensible in his present state of development. These beings have been active in the creation of the world and man. They have created the solar system and all that belongs thereto. They have developed Earth and man to their present state. Some have now withdrawn from active participation; others are still at work.

Each rank has three members. In the following schedule the various names are given, some of which are characteristic of the particular activity of that being.

The Godhead

First Hierarchy	Seraphim, Spirits of Love Cherubim, Spirits of Harmony Thrones, Spirits of Will
Second Hierarchy	Kyriotetes, Spirits of Wisdom, Dominions Dynamis, Spirits of Motion, Virtues, Mights Exusiai, Spirits of Form, Powers, Revelations (In Hebrew the equivalent of Exusiai is Elohim)
Third Hierarchy	Archai, Spirits of Personality, Primal Beginnings, Principalities Archangeloi, Spirits of Fire, Archangels Angeloi, Sons of Life, Sons of Twilight, Angels

Like man, the Hierarchies are also engaged in a process of evolution. Like man, they evolve through their work and experience. Like man, they develop at different rates. At each stage of development some members of the Hierarchies fail to reach the goal or purposely forego a normal development. There are thus a whole series of retarded beings who might be termed Spirits of Adversity. They are not evil in themselves but they provide adverse influences with which man has to deal.

The human being is, therefore, exposed to the forces of advancement and retardation, of good and evil, of God and the devil.

In the process of human development man changes from being a receiver to being a giver. As a child he receives; as an adult, he gives. The evolution of the Hierarchies follows this pattern. At first they receive; later they are in a position to give. Thus the highest Hierarchies can give of their substance to create the world and man. The lower ones work under their direction and in so doing further their own development.

The Work of the Hierarchies in Creation

Vol. 2, chapter 1 of this work deals with the development of the solar system, including, of course, the Earth. The agencies behind this development are the Hierarchies, who also create man.

As in a single life-span the human being first receives, then gives, so in the whole process of evolution man's path of development is from being created to becoming a creator. In very rough outline it can be said that the Hierarchies provide substance, then impulse and stimuli to awaken activity. The activity is transformed into inner life which then proceeds under its own impetus and becomes creative. Man will become 'like God'.

An enormous flexibility and stretch of mind is necessary to grasp these matters even in an elementary way. A fundamental thought to hold in mind is that in the world around us are the preserved thoughts of the gods.

Initially, the highest members of the First Hierarchy, the Seraphim, receive the impulse from the Godhead to create man and an environment in which he can evolve, i.e. the solar system. They contemplate the world-to-be but their contemplation is at the same time a creative act that brings a world into existence in a purely spiritual form. One might look upon it as an 'idea' world. The Cherubim have the task of transforming the ideas into workable plans and bringing them into harmony with other systems in the universe. The third group of the First Hierarchy, the Thrones, puts the plans into practice and provides the initial substance.

Although it sounds somewhat trite in view of the magnificent work of creation, the members of the Second Hierarchy, i.e. the Kyriotetes, Dynamis and Exusiai, are the artisans of the solar system. The members of the First Hierarchy are so far evolved that they are in a position to be creators, i.e. to give or to sacrifice. What they give constitutes an initial stage. The Second Hierarchy takes over, to form a system according to plan, to maintain it and to begin work on the formation of the human physical body.

The members of the Third Hierarchy, under the guidance of the higher ranks, work on the human being-to-be. They mould and remould the prototype substance which will one day house an independent human spirit; they provide stimuli to awaken inner experiences such as feeling and thinking. The object is to create a being (man) whose goal of evolution is independence.

To understand this it has to be appreciated that by their very nature the higher Hierarchies merely reflect the Divinity. They have no freedom and the question of freedom does not arise. The destiny of man is different. He is to gain new and enhanced faculties by struggling with adversity caused by the left-behind members of the Hierarchies. At the same time this gives him the possibility of falling into error. It is part of the divine plan that he shall work out his own salvation, that he shall eventually evolve through his own efforts. In the course of aeons man will become the Tenth Hierarchy in his own right, because he will have earned it.

The work of creation is so remote from our present day thinking that it is very difficult to imagine. Two lines of thought may help to understand it.

One is to consider the different states of matter, i.e. solids, liquids, gases. On Earth we have a very common substance which appears in all three forms. Under the right conditions ice turns to water and water to steam. With four elements in mind we might imagine a further stage of attenuation, namely, warmth. Looking at the process the other way round, one would have a process of condensation—warmth, gas, liquid, solid. In the course of evolution an emanation of a particular kind of warmth became matter, i.e. spiritual substance crystallized into the physical.

A second consideration which might be helpful is to consider a plant. To form its roots, leaves, flowers and seeds, a plant needs physical substances; it needs light, air and water. But there is something in the plant that transcends all these, namely, that which gives it its particular form and shape but which is not ordinarily perceptible. Only one step is necessary to say that there is a spiritual entity manifesting itself in physical form.

The first stage of Earth development or the solar system is known as Ancient Saturn, or the Saturn-condition, and this can be imagined as a huge sphere of warmth in space which reached as far as the orbit of the present planet Saturn, taking the Sun as the centre. But it was not warmth in our modern sense. One might call it spiritual warmth. It was 'will' substance, poured out by the third member of the First Hierarchy, the Thrones. They provided the initial substance already referred to, but again this 'substance' did not have substantiality as we understand it today. It was into this substance of the Thrones that other beings worked in order to create a foundation for man's physical body.

Looked at purely anatomically and physiologically, the human being is a marvellous piece of work, but the physical body is the bearer of other attributes. It is endowed with a life force (etheric body); it is the physical expression of a soul (astral body); it is the instrument of the individuality (ego). In its construction, therefore, all these points must have been taken into consideration. In order that man could develop according to the ideas of the Godhead, the physical body had to be endowed with many potentialities. In fairy stories we have the picture of the fairies endowing the baby with various qualities. In the story of creation it is the Hierarchies who bestow the gifts.

In Ancient Saturn the human body was not physical as we understand it today. We can think of it as a prototype, malleable and flexible, still existing only in spirit. It had to be formed, shaped and worked into, so that it would be capable of bearing and using the gifts that it would eventually receive. Thus the various capacities were implanted into it in embryo form.

At this stage the members of the highest Hierarchy func-
tioned from outside the globe of warmth in the region we now
call the zodiac. Ancient Saturn had an 'atmosphere' of spiritual beings. One has to imagine their influence radiating in
from the whole circle but differentiated according to the
direction from which it comes. That is to say, the influence
was modified by the forces of the different regions of the
zodiac.

These hierarchical influences laid the first foundation for
the form of the different parts of the body, i.e. head, throat,
heart, lungs, etc. Remnants of this knowledge were still current in the Middle Ages when it was considered that Aries (the
Ram) and the head were connected; Taurus (the Bull) and the
throat; Leo (the Lion), the heart, etc.

The Second and Third Hierarchies were active not from the
outside but within the body of warmth. From among the
members of the Second Hierarchy the Kyriotetes had to
translate the commands and impulses from their superiors
into reality, the Dynamis provided the necessary continuity of
activity and the Exusiai maintained what was achieved. They
had a task with regard to man.

It was stated that the physical body had to have the possibility of bearing an etheric, an astral and an ego. The Thrones
having provided the substance, it was the turn of the Kyriotetes who radiated their forces into it so that it could sub-
sequently take up an etheric body. The Dynamis did the same
for the astral and the Exusiai for the ego. These were only
preliminary steps.

The beings of the Third Hierarchy had other tasks. The
Archai furthered the process of differentiation that resulted in
a basis for personality. The result of the work of the Archangels was to produce the germinal organs of sense while the
Angels worked on the germinal organs of nutrition and bodily
function.

After a time a certain stage of completion was reached
beyond which no further progress could be made in the given
conditions. Hence the Thrones, who were the chief guides of
Ancient Saturn, now dissolved it.

A new sphere had to be created with new guidance. Before

this could be constituted there was a period of rest, known as pralaya, the equivalent of sleep in human life.

To understand the next phase one might consider what happens when something burns. Heat is produced and the warmth splits into two elements. Something like this process happened to produce the next planetary development. The warmth of Saturn split into light and smoke (or gas). The reconstituted sphere was, however, smaller and forces were left outside which became the basis of the present planet Saturn. Its extent was from the present Sun to the orbit of Jupiter, and, because light was a feature of it, it is known as Ancient Sun or the Sun-condition. It was a radiant gaseous body. The Kyriotetes were the chief guides in this phase. They had been instrumental in condensing the substance of Ancient Saturn to Ancient Sun. The Spirits of Form, in their own evolution, were now able to relinquish their etheric body. The Kyriotetes worked this etheric substance, this life-force, together with a contribution from themselves, into the prototype physical bodies of man-in-the-making, having previously prepared them to receive it. One could say that at this point the human being was in a sort of plant stage. Not all the substance of Ancient Saturn had been irradiated so that in Ancient Sun there was another kingdom, the prototype mineral world.

Thus at this stage there were two kingdoms of nature but not as we now know them.

It must be borne in mind that through their activity the higher beings also evolved. They had therefore the possibility of becoming more effective. What was achieved in Ancient Saturn on the making of man now had to be modified in view of the new conditions and the bestowal of the etheric. Thus all the potentialities that were implanted in the Saturn stage were now transformed to a new level.

Again there was a withdrawal period and again a re-awakening. The Dynamis transformed Ancient Sun to Ancient Moon and they were now the chief agencies. The gaseous substance of Ancient Sun was condensed to something of a liquid consistency. The contracted sphere extended as far as the orbit of Mars and it is known as Ancient Mars or Ancient

Moon. Again a residue of forces were left outside which manifested later as the planet Jupiter.

(In speaking of gas or liquid it must be borne in mind that these are not the same as our present gases or liquids. One still has to think of them as of the nature of prototypes. The use of the word 'Moon' may cause some confusion. Ancient Moon is not in any way to be equated with our present Moon. It is possible that it derives this appellation from the fact that members of the Dynamis were at different stages of evolution and a division took place in the Ancient Mars—or Ancient Moon—sphere. The more advanced members formed one colony which could be called a sort of sun and the less advanced formed another, a satellite which revolved around it. Eventually the two were united again.)

As far as the development of man is concerned, the astral was now incorporated into the combined human physical and etheric bodies. The Dynamis now gave of their own essence together with the etheric released by the evolving Exusiai and the human-being-to-be was therefore now endowed with a third principle. Again in the changed environment and with the new powers there was more work for the Hierarchies in adapting and transforming.

One could say that the human being was now at the animal stage. Not all the substance received the astral and there was therefore now a prototype plant world as well as the mineral.

After another pralaya the fourth period of development began and this brought with it further contraction and condensation. The Earth as we now know it was not in existence and the new sphere still contained what was later our present Sun, Earth with its Moon, and the minor planets. (See vol. 2, chapter 1 of this work.) Forces left outside the new sphere formed, in due course, the planet Mars.

A similar process to what had happened before now took place. The Hierarchies themselves had developed further, conditions had changed and all qualities and organs appertaining to the human being had to be metamorphosed. It was during this period that what was spiritual now became manifest as physical matter and that the physical organism of man was created. The totally new endowment that he received was the ego, a gift from the Exusiai, a drop of their own substance.

Those entities not sufficiently mature to receive the ego formed the future animal world.

Before dealing with this cosmic body of combined Sun, Earth and minor planets, it may be helpful to look back at the formation of what we now see as Saturn, Jupiter, Mars.

The fact was already mentioned that certain beings do not complete their evolution. The normal Spirits of Form (Exusiai) set the boundaries of the spheres, i.e. Ancient Saturn, Ancient Sun (Jupiter), Ancient Moon (Mars), but the abnormal ones are banished or remain outside and work from outside. Thus at each stage of contraction there is a disturbance at the periphery which becomes manifest in the course of further development as a planet. This then is the home of a colony of beings who have fallen out of the normal stream.

The undifferentiated cosmic body which later split into Sun, Earth and the minor planets became denser, but for man, whose further evolution was to be through contact with a material world, it was not yet dense enough. For some beings, members of the Exusiai, the environment was unsuitable and for their further development they withdraw, together with subordinate beings through whom they act, and formed what is our present Sun. Others were not sufficiently mature to accompany them yet were too far advanced to remain within the changing conditions. They were at an intermediate stage and the two planets Mercury and Venus split off as their habitations.

There now remained a contracted sphere consisting of present Earth and Moon combined.

The Spirits of Form, the Exusiai (the Elohim of the Hebrews) are essentially connected with Earth evolution. Not only are they concerned with man but they are the ones who give the planet its configuration. It is at the beginning of the Bible that we read: 'In the beginning God created the heaven and the earth.' But for 'God' one should read 'Elohim', as it is in the original.

Those members of the Hierarchy who had made their

dwelling place in the Sun now sent down their influence from that direction but, had there been no counterforce, this would have resulted in an unbalanced development in man's evolution. To prevent this one of the Exusiai stayed with the Earth, and when, due to other adverse influences, the Earth was tending towards too great a densification, he took the grossest forces out, the result of which was the formation of our present Moon. The human being now lives in a state of balance between the promoting forces of the Sun and the retarding effect of the Moon.

(The roles of Christ and Jehovah are connected with these matters.)

At our present stage of evolution man has been endowed by the Hierarchies with physical, etheric and astral bodies, and an ego. He has been given the Earth as his work place and a cosmic setting. The world is an expression of the thoughts and deeds of spiritual beings but the beings themselves are no longer actively engaged in creation although their influence is still effective in certain areas. The world is now, so to speak, complete. Man is responsible for it and for his own further evolution but he will receive help from the higher beings if he seeks it in the right way. This means a development of his own spiritual faculties.

The Third Hierarchy, those beings more closely connected with the human being, are still with us.

The Spheres of the Hierarchies

With our Earth-bound thinking there are always difficulties in trying to visualize conditions in the spiritual world. Yet earthly concepts must be used to try to attain some understanding. A question which may arise is that concerning the dwelling place of the Hierarchies.

A short answer would be to say 'in the spiritual world'. But the spiritual world is a general term covering many regions. The regions can be equated with the planetary spheres.

In speaking of regions, however, and of spiritual beings, one must remember that space in the spiritual world does not have the same quality as in the physical. Spiritual spaces, like spiritual beings, are interpenetrating and this is something to be remembered when what is described is given in spatial concepts. Spiritual realms do not exist side by side but inter-mingle with one another. If a human being can attain spiritual vision, the regions become progressively perceptible as his ability increases.

With our normal consciousness we look into the apparently endless blue sky by day and interminable blackness by night in which are scattered the innumerable points of light repre-senting stars and planets and we think in terms of physical objects. But perhaps we must call an imaginative faculty into play and picture these vast spaces inhabited by countless beings whose influence radiates down to us just as the warmth of the Sun.

Looking back a little into history we note that, at the time of the Middle Ages, a new concept of the universe came into men's minds. The centre of the universe was shifted from the Earth to the Sun and the planets revolved around it according to mechanical laws. Stars and planets became physical objects only. In still earlier times, in Atlantean or in the early cultures of post-Atlantean times (Ancient India to Greece), people had a different understanding. They were aware of spiritual beings in the cosmos, and when the names of the planets were used they were understood as centres or spheres of spiritual activity. As late as the time of St Paul, his intimate pupil, Dionysius the Areopagite, proclaimed that spiritual beings lived in space and that the soul could develop to a perception of them.

Since the time of Copernicus (1473–1543) we have come to look upon the Sun as the centre of the solar system, with the planets, including the Earth and its satellite, moving around it. The older point of view, commonly known as the Ptolemaic, is the one where the Earth is considered the centre, with the Moon, Sun and the planets circling around it. This is the apparent movement from our Earth. Thinking of the spheres of the planets in connection with the spiritual Hierarchies, the Ptolemaic view is correct. If one considers also the fact that the Earth is the present scene of man's evolution in the whole of planetary development, a central position may be accorded it.

Whether one considers the attitude of the ancient peoples or of modern initiates, to both of them the cosmos is full of perceptible beings and within the planetary orbits are the spatial dwellings of the Hierarchies. The Moon orbits the Earth, and taking the Earth as centre and the circular path of the Moon around it one can visualize a sphere in space. This is interpenetrated by the spheres of which other planets form the orbits.

Thus there are a series of concentric spheres and it is here that the various higher beings have their habitations. The orbits mark out the limits of the realms of rulership of each member of each Hierarchy.

Although a certain sphere is the home of certain higher beings, it does not mean that they only function there. For instance the Spirits of Form have a common centre in the Sun sphere but they set the boundaries of the outer planets and also work within the spheres thus enclosed.

Sphere:	Inhabitated by:
Moon	Angels
Mercury	Archangels
Venus	Archai
Sun	Exusiai
Mars	Dynamis
Jupiter	Kyriotetes
Saturn	Thrones

Beyond Saturn is the region of the Cherubim and Seraphim, in the zodiac.

(It should be noted that in the course of history the names of Mercury and Venus have been exchanged. What is called Mercury above is the present Venus and Venus above is the present astronomical Mercury.)

There are planets beyond Saturn, e.g. Uranus and Neptune, but these do not properly belong to the solar system. They were formed by beings who had already withdrawn from Ancient Saturn.

Hierarchies, Earth and Man

In the physical world we distinguish various natural kingdoms. Below man, in descending order, are the animal, plant and mineral worlds, the three kingdoms of nature. In the spiritual world are the kingdoms of the Hierarchies. Above man, in ascending order, are the three ranks of higher beings. The nearest to man is the Third Hierarchy whose members are the Angels, Archangels and the Archai and who are essentially concerned with man's development.

One stage further developed than man are the Angels. They have no physical body and no need to incarnate. The Angels have the task of watching over man and guiding him in certain matters for which he himself as yet does not have the capacity.

One example is the fairly common experience that some unseen power seems to guide us on occasion. We do things unconsciously and yet, looking back on life, it can be felt that we were led in some particular direction that was not intended at the time. We speak of a Guardian Angel, or a Guiding Spirit.

Another is that in his present imperfect condition man is not yet master of himself. He has control of only part of his astral body, which is the seat of desires, urges and impulses. In the course of time he will transform it so that it becomes a higher member of his being and he gains a new faculty. It is one of the tasks of the Angel to help man in this work.

Normally a man is not aware of his Guardian Angel although a sense of the presence of this higher being may sometimes be discerned in the soul in particular circumstances. When, for instance, a human being fulfils a task out of pure love, entirely beyond egoistical interests, then he may become aware of some supersensible agency, which is in fact his Guardian Angel.

The Archangels are not concerned with individuals but with groups of people, e.g. nations. The expression 'folk-soul' or 'folk-spirit', although generally used in an abstract sense, can be taken to indicate a reality. The Archangels are the guiding spirits of particular nations or peoples. It is also their task to govern the relationship between individuals and the nation or people.

The next rank is that of the Archai, the Primal Beginnings, or the Spirits of Personality. Whereas Angels are concerned with individuals and Archangels with race, the Archai have the guidance of a whole epoch as their mission. The expression 'Spirit of the Times' can also be taken as a reality. The Archai have the task of guiding a particular period which is not restricted to a particular people. One can think in terms of cultural epochs such as those of Egypt/Chaldea/Babylon/Assyria or Greece/Rome. The Archai influence the incarnation of certain personalities whose presence on Earth is necessary at these particular times.

In the course of history members of the above Hierarchy have had special tasks under special circumstances.

If we think back to ancient times before man received the ego, humanity could be compared with children who need guidance. Before the Earth solidified into its present condition it went through other stages, where, in tune with its development, the human structure was less rigid than it is today. The period immediately preceding our own was Atlantis, and the one before that Lemuria. In these periods mankind was directly led by beings of the Third Hierarchy. Archai, Archangels and Angels acted through human agency. The people felt the influence of divine spiritual beings who inspired but did not directly incarnate. There were, however, other members of the Hierarchy who had fallen behind in their development and did incarnate, of which more will be said later.

In Lemuria there was no speech and no thinking as we understand it and hence no communication as we know it. Certain members of the Archai permeated particular human bodies and radiated an influence from the spiritual worlds that people accepted instinctively.

In Atlantis Archangels worked through human beings who were centred in the oracles and were the priests of the age. Manu (Noah) was such a one.

In late Atlantis and into the first periods of post-Atlantean civilizations, Angels were the main inspirers, although there are some cases of the presence of Archai and Archangels.

Although no longer active in creation, the higher Hierarchies still have tasks to fulfil. It has been described elsewhere how the Earth is one of a series of planetary developments. The Exusiai have the task of seeing that humanity passes rightly from one stage to the next. The Earth is the place where man works out his karma at present. It has a particular form. For this also, the Exusiai, the Spirits of Form, are the responsible beings. But within the form there is continual movement. In the limited period of a lifetime the relative positions of land and sea may not change greatly but over a longer period the changing relationships are to be observed. An example is the change in the configuration of the Earth from Atlantis to the present time. Water and air are in continual motion. Moisture is drawn upwards, clouds form and rain falls. The explanation of such matters as given by physics may be correct as far as it goes, but there are also more subtle influences. These continual movements in the planet may be likened to the etheric body of man. They are an expression of life and are brought about by the Dynamis, the Spirits of Motion. Behind the form and behind the movement is a sort of awareness of what must happen. This idea, this consciousness, is invested in the Kyriotetes, the Spirits of Wisdom.

The Earth, however, is not on its own. It belongs to the rest of the solar system and to the universe. It obeys certain laws and the agencies governing its path through space are the Thrones, the Spirits of Will. To harmonize its movement with the rest of the planets is the task of the Cherubim, the Spirits of Harmony, while the Seraphim, the Spirits of Love, regulate the functioning of the solar system with other systems.

At all stages there are members of the Hierarchies whose development is incomplete and man lives both under the influence of the normal beings and of those who have remained behind. These were termed Spirits of Adversity but it must be remembered that they are not evil in themselves.

As man grows in strength by overcoming obstacles, the Divinity saw fit to make his path less straightforward than it might have been in order that he should develop new qualities. Certain members of the Hierarchies were prevailed upon, or allowed, to remain behind in their development. It was a sacrifice. Their action furthered the interests of man but at the same time introduced the possibility of evil.

It is the nature of Angels to reflect the activities of higher
ranking beings, and when some of these renounced further
development some Angels followed their example. They
received an impulse to be free, to develop an inner life themselves. They are known as Luciferic beings.

Owing to their changed condition they needed a different
means of gaining experience and found that a closer connection with man could provide this. This affected man in such a
way that he received astral forces which he could not entirely
control. Thus although his feelings can give rise to noble
endeavour they can also be devoted to selfish ends. Unless
checked and guided by a higher element in his being, man's
passions, urges and impulses can lead to fanaticism and to a
state of mind where he is not in control of himself. The power
of the Luciferic spirits is thus strengthened. They would like to
rule the world.

The Luciferic beings persuaded man that he could become
independent of divine powers. They gave him a new faculty
and he became aware of the physical world. His eyes were
opened. Prior to this he had lived in a state of consciousness of
the spiritual world and thus was unconscious of bodily functions. Now he became aware of the process of propagation,
aware of sickness, pain and death.

There is a purpose for man in being influenced by abnormal
beings but what at a certain time is progressive for him
becomes retrogressive if continued into a later period under
different conditions. For humanity's wider experience and
development diversity was essential. Thus at one stage the
Luciferic spirits divided mankind into races. For a time that
was perfectly justified but if extended beyond a certain period
then negative symptoms appear such as racialism and
nationalism.

It was said earlier that in Lemurian and Atlantean times
beings of the Third Hierarchy permeated human bodies and
were revered leaders, but there were also some who actually
fully incarnated. They were the ones whose development was
incomplete and they held a middle position between man and
Angel. They became humanity's teachers and founders of
different civilizations.

In Lemurian times speech was prompted by the normal Angels and would have been uniform throughout mankind, but Luciferic beings incarnated into particular groups of people and taught particular languages.

Contact with the physical world brought another danger to man. Besides the Luciferic beings there are others known usually by the name given to them in the Persian epoch, Ahrimanic or Spirits of Darkness.

It is not the intention here to deal with the problem of good and evil or the matter of redemption which includes the mission of the Christ, but some brief indication of these things must be given in the context of the general theme.

While the Luciferic forces would draw man away from the Earth, those of Ahriman would bind him closer to it. It is the object of the latter to persuade man that the material world is the only one that matters.

With these two powers man must contend. To help him to combat them a mighty spiritual Being came to Earth and incarnated in a human body, bringing revitalizing powers into the Earth's atmosphere whereby man can strengthen his ego forces, purify his astral and recognize the physical world as a manifestation of the spiritual. This was the Christ. He did not seek to coerce. No higher power can force man to do good. Man is to rise and be free through his own effort and eventually redeem his adversaries.

There is another very important connection between the Hierarchies and man, namely, their meeting which takes place during man's period of sleep and in the time between death and rebirth. There is, or should be, a mutually beneficial exchange of experiences.

A careful observer in these matters might discern occasionally a certain uneasy feeling on waking, something akin to a bad conscience. This may be due to an unsatisfactory meeting with the higher beings. The reason for this may lie in what has been spoken the previous day. Speech and its content are not only of importance in physical life but have far wider implications.

What has been spoken by the human being during the day re-echoes in the spiritual world in sleep and should bring joy to certain members of the Hierarchies. But slovenly speech and materialistic content bring no pleasure and this in turn inhibits the higher beings from giving certain invigorating forces. Thus the human being suffers a form of deprivation.

Furthermore, the Hierarchies themselves then suffer from a sort of undernourishment. What the human being takes into the spiritual world is of consequence for them. They cannot give if they do not receive and this is particularly important for man in his journey through the spheres after death. It is the task of the spiritual beings in the heavenly regions to transform human deeds and work the results into the new karma which will be experienced in subsequent incarnations. The Third Hierarchy is concerned with the formation of the body; the Second implants forces of attraction and aversion, which are a guide to find related human beings; the First Hierarchy helps to determine the path which leads to events and apparent happenings.

It must be remembered that what the human being says and does is not only his affair and that of the Hierarchies but it affects the world in general.

The Hierarchies in Nature

With our normal consciousness we live in a physical world, but this is only a half-existence. The physical world is a manifestation of spiritual forces. If our minds were sufficiently developed we should perceive these forces not as abstractions but as higher beings.

We speak of a physical Earth and physical effects but the Earth is subject to all sorts of influences streaming in from the cosmos. The effect of Sun and Moon are well recognized and certain planetary influences can be demonstrated, but we can now think a little further to whole ranks of spiritual beings in space who also radiate something into our Earth.

When we consider man, we see first his physical body. There is, however, something in the physical body which keeps it alive—a supersensible principle or body known as the etheric.

There is something further which is the seat of urge and impulse—the astral—and beyond that the overriding guide which we call the ego.

With regard to the Earth, there is a similar arrangement but what we term principles or bodies are beings. These beings are the Hierarchies and their offspring or servants.

The Earth has an obvious physical existence. In so far as there is life in the physical, it has an etheric. Some force provides impulses and stimulation. This is the astral, and there is a certain guiding power which we can equate with the ego.

Let us consider the kingdoms of nature below man, i.e. mineral, plant and animal. The mineral is usually thought of as dead matter and from a certain aspect this is correct. But matter is something which has crystallized out of being, and if we think back to the origins of Ancient Saturn then we may appreciate that what has become matter is a part of the warmth substance that emanated from a member of the highest Hierarchy, the Thrones. In the case of the mineral the substance was not further vitalized but it still possesses form and inner being. Metals have definite characteristics; rocks are composed of various substances which give each a unique character. The plant world represents a further stage of development. It has an endless array of form and manner of growth. The animal world is further advanced and has equally a multitude of differentiations.

Once the Earth was created, it required a sustaining and maintaining element. The active forces that gave the mineral its inner being, the plant its unique shape and movement, and each animal species its particular characteristic stream down from the heavenly spheres, the dwelling places of the Hierarchies, but for their work on Earth the Hierarchies have assistants.

In the solid substance, in the rocks, in the metals are the so-called earth spirits. In the mist, cloud and spray are the water spirits. The latter are the beings whose task it is to draw the plant upward from the earth. Around the blossom and fruit of the plant hover the beings of air while a fourth category transmutes the warmth of the environment into the ripening forces.

It is the co-operation of all the nature spirits that forms the etheric body of the Earth and the nature spirits are helpers and offspring of the Third Hierarchy. As a plant puts forth seed, so the Hierarchies can produce other beings. The difference is that a plant will grow like its parent but the offspring of the Hierarchy does not attain the same status.

Behind the activity of the Third Hierarchy is that of the Second, which provides stimulus. The fact that everything has form, the world and all its inhabitants, was already mentioned. Of form there is an endless variety. Form changes, however, in the process of growth. We need only think of the metamorphosis of the plant, how seed changes to leaf, leaf to flower, flower to fruit and fruit to seed. In animal and man there is change and growth but in all these developments there is innate wisdom.

In creation the Second Hierarchy was concerned with bestowing the astral on man and the Second Hierarchy have offspring in the astral world. These are the group souls of plants and animals.

(Group soul or group ego may require a little explanation. In man we recognize an individual and attribute human individuality to the ego. Each person is an individuality in his own right but this does not apply to the plant or animal kingdom. Although a single animal may have its idiosyncrasies, we note that its nature and behaviour is very similar to every other animal of that species in fundamentals. Yet each species is individual and therefore one can speak of the individuality of a species, known otherwise as the group soul or group ego. The same applies to plants.)

Also in the astral sphere, giving directions to the nature spirits, are other beings who are the offspring of the First Hierarchy.

The First Hierarchy consists—so to speak—of directors, originators. As the human being lives in certain rhythms, for instance the rhythmical change between sleeping and waking, so does the Earth. There are forces that influence the blossoming and withering of plants, the alternation of day and night, the changing seasons, the life-span of animals. These forces emanate from the First Hierarchy but they are administered by their offspring, known as the Spirits of Rotation of Time. These beings govern everything that takes place in the rhythms of nature, everything that depends on repeated happenings.

We could summarize then the influence of the Hierarchies in nature as follows, remembering the intermediaries:

In the forces of the elements	Third Hierarchy
In the form and metamorphosis	Second Hierarchy
In the origins of laws and rhythms	First Hierarchy

When the human being uses his senses (i.e. sight, hearing, smell, taste, touch), he becomes aware of objects in the physical world. He may make thoughts about these objects with regard to their forces, laws and even causes, but in the final instance objects have 'being' and this is a spiritual entity. At some future stage of his evolution man will develop new capacities that will give him an awareness of the Hierarchies while he is still an inhabitant of the physical world.

3

THE PHILOSOPHICAL APPROACH
TO THE SPIRIT

Each to the whole its substance gives,
Each in the other works and lives.

Goethe, through the voice of Faust, is expressing here the
fact that the world is a unity, that the parts make up a whole,
that the whole is the sum of the parts, that everything is
connected in some way with everything else.

Our gaze may fall on the plant world. It does not exist for
itself alone. It purifies the air, provides food for man and beast
and other essentials for the needs of man. But it can only exist
in conjunction with other elements. It needs soil in which to
grow, nutrients in the soil, water, air, light and warmth.

We may look up to the heavens and note the orderly procession of Sun, Moon and stars, all of which have some
relationship to the Earth.

Science points to the remarkable fact that in the evolution of
the Earth just those things appeared which made life possible.
It is, however, conceivable that had other elements been
deposited, another form of life would have developed. In any
case these facts point to unity.

The human being is also a product of nature. His physical
body is made up of the ingredients of nature. When he has
finished with it, it disintegrates into natural substances.
Throughout his life man is bound up with and dependent on
the natural world. He needs the firm earth on which to tread,
the products of earth for his sustenance, air to breathe, light
and warmth.

Yet when the human being begins to reflect about himself,

he experiences a duality. On the one hand there is the natural world to which he is obviously related, yet a consciousness of self tells him that he is something apart. The questions arise: Can this dichotomy be resolved? Is it possible to overcome this feeling of separation? Is there a point at which unity is established?

Let us consider again the grand tableau of the natural world. Not only is there unity but there is also order. Life follows a certain pattern, the constellations revolve in definite sequence, the Sun rises and sets regularly. Have all these arrangements happened accidentally or are we led to think of some design in the universe. We may observe the functioning of a piece of mechanism but behind it lies the thought or the idea of the inventor. Similarly we can consider the world and the universe and infer that behind the manifestation lies a thought or an idea but these are emanations of the Divine Mind.

If man is really one with the world then not only are there corresponding physical factors but there must be something within man to correspond to the Divine Thought. At our present stage of evolution this is human thought.

The outside world and the body of man are one. The same substances are in nature as in the body. Man's thoughts also exist in nature. They are the spiritual background. The thoughts man thinks are everywhere in the world outside. He is not conscious of this due to the limitations of his development but he can aspire to greater consciousness.

The Evolution of Thinking

The capacity to think is a relatively late development in human evolution. The year 600 BC, or thereabouts, saw the birth of philosophy and this marks a new way of thinking. At the same time the feeling of ego-consciousness grew stronger. Peoples of previous civilizations had not experienced themselves so strongly as individuals but more as members of a family, race or tribe. In ancient Egypt, Persia, India, the mind of man had been differently constituted. The people of those times had been aware of spirituality in the universe. They had experienced spiritual beings in the cosmos. Sun, Moon and stars had possessed spiritual qualities. Nature was endowed with spirit. The background of the natural world came to them as revelation, either direct or through the Mystery schools.

(The Mystery schools were a sort of church and university combined but the leaders were initiates and the pupils learned to appreciate and perceive spiritual forces behind the world of matter, becoming initiates themselves. The influence of the Mystery schools permeated general culture.)

The faculty of spiritual perception began to disappear in Greek times and thinking took its place.

When the human being awakens to a consciousness of self, questions begin to arise in his soul as to his place in the world, his connections with the rest of the world and of his ultimate destiny. The questions arise as a need of the soul. There is a parallel to this experience in childhood when the emerging individuality begins to seek its way in life. There arises then a striving for knowledge, that particular form of knowledge which can satisfy the need.

Among the Greek philosophers Aristotle is outstanding. He taught his pupils to observe and to relate their thinking to their observation. He was the founder of logic and he inaugurated that way of thinking which leads step by step to knowledge. Aristotle spoke of 'form' and 'matter'. Today we should use other expressions but what he had in mind was that our initial knowledge is provided by sense impressions of objects. These represent the 'matter'. But when we begin to think we arrive at the 'form'. The 'form' is the vital principle. It expresses the universal. The 'matter' which is perceived through the senses is the individual object.

In the course of history the faculty of logical thinking concentrates on the material world. The centre of culture shifts to Europe and in the sixteenth century thought takes a noticeable step in the direction of materialism.

As late as medieval times the Earth was considered the centre of the heavens and everything had a purpose connected with man. The new age is heralded by scientists such as

Francis Bacon, Galileo and Harvey. It is now assumed that only sense-observation of nature is reliable. Galileo works at the laws of physics, invents a telescope and the planets are no longer the homes of spiritual beings but bodies of matter, like our own Earth, hurtling through space. Bacon trains himself to observe the material phenomena, to experiment and to deduce laws in conformity with physical aspects. Harvey dissects the human body, makes outstanding discoveries but interprets the bodily activities mechanistically. The heart is seen as a pump and organic processes are interpreted mechanically.

Newton (1643–1727) discovered the laws of motion and universal gravitation. He worked out the laws of the tides and improved the telescope. He formulated the mechanics of the universe. He suggested that the solar system kept going by its own momentum. He allowed that perhaps the planets had been hurled into space by God in the first instance but then were left to their own momentum. Newton confirmed mathematically the quite new concept of the planetary system, proclaimed by Galileo and Kepler, in which the Earth had become a planet revolving around the Sun with many others. The spiritual agencies of the universe were negated, colours and sounds became 'vibrations'—in short, scientists came to the conclusion that everything was explainable in terms of mechanics or physics.

And what of man? He too was involved. Man lost his cosmic status and it was anticipated that he also could be explained in terms of the material and mathematical.

The change in outlook is also recognizable in the philosophers of the period. In the new age human thought begins to be considered as something outside nature and it becomes necessary to make thought valid through its own strength. Descartes produced the famous dictum 'Cogito, ergo sum' (I think, therefore I am) and he argued the two independent worlds of mind and body.

Now various philosophic 'systems' develop, the crucial problems of which are based on this duality. Spinoza builds purely on thought. He attempts to build up a system of philosophy as Euclid had constructed a system of geometry, by a chain of reasoning depending on definitions and axioms. Leibniz cannot accept as truth anything that appears in the outside world. His picture of the world is one which is formed by the inner energy of the self-conscious soul.

(The reader wishing to explore all the philosophical points in depth is recommended to study Rudolf Steiner's work *The Riddles of Philosophy*, which is the basis for most of what appears in this chapter.)

In England we have the philosophies of the Empiricists—knowledge is based on experience. Locke says that all our knowledge is ultimately derived from experience. The soul cannot have any knowledge except that which it derives from interaction with the outer world. Hume believes that only sense impressions and rational observations can be true; any ideas that men form above and beyond these can only exist as belief. But we also have the philosophy of Bishop Berkeley for whom all knowledge is mental—I can know nothing of the things outside; I can only know of the impressions that the things make on me.

Of great impact in the thinking world was Kant. He is one who realized that speculation is not fruitful and he wished for certainty in the field of philosophy. He put the question: What can I know? He maintained that the world outside only affects us through observation. How, therefore, can there be anything certain for us through this observation. The mind builds the world according to its own constitution. Mathematics and science contain only the laws of our own mental organization. This, when explored, gives absolute truth. Reason does not draw its laws from nature; it dictates them to nature. The mind, however, is stimulated from outside to develop its inner world, and therefore there must be something in the outer world. This is the 'thing-in-itself', but we can know nothing of such things-in-themselves except that they exist. What we can know does not refer to real things outside but to processes within ourselves. For Kant the ultimate reality of nature remains outside man. Man can only know or experience nature through the formulations of his mind.

But what of God? Immortality? Freedom? These are not observable but they exist within the mind and give rise to our state of soul. But these things we cannot know. We apprehend them through the voice of duty (categorical imperative). Kant believes that the soul is free to follow the inner voice of duty. This is morality. In the soul, as in nature, human knowledge comes to a halt. The laws of human reasoning apply only to the inner world of the mind.

Into this whirlpool of ideas and counter-ideas comes Goethe. In direct opposition to Kant, he declares that we can know everything. For Goethe the spirit of man is wholly in nature because nature herself is spirit.

We shall refer to Goethe later.

In 1859 a work was published that was to have a tremendous impact. This was Darwin's book on evolution, *The Origin of Species by Means of Natural Selection or the Preservation of Favoured Races in the Struggle for Life.*

It contributed greatly to the materialistic conception of man which predominates in today's culture. It used to be thought than an omniscient, all-powerful Being created man with the words 'Let us make man in our own image'. We humans were at the centre of things; we were known by God and loved by Him. We addressed Him as 'Our Father'.

But modern science has changed all that. It indicates that there was never any purpose in creation but what has taken place in evolution is a series of accidents. The origins of the Earth go back to some accidental happenings in the cosmos that resulted in the creation of a planet on which by chance the physical conditions were suitable to make life possible as we know it. Then special compounds came into existence having the property of livingness. Living matter, having brought itself forth, maintained itself. Different forms evolved from stage to stage, leading finally to man. What had been a creation in God's image became something arising from the primeval mud.

. Let it be said that this materialistic outlook did not originate with Darwin himself. Darwin contented himself with stating the sequence of facts as they appeared to him. It was his followers who drew the conclusions that man had evolved in this way.

But there were still thinkers concerned with the process of

knowing. They were still concerned with the nature of reality. Does reality lie in the objects of the world or is it existent only in the mind? John Stuart Mill builds his philosophy on the recognition and comparison of facts and observable phenomena but can find no absolute distinction between mind and matter. He allows that this mode of thinking does not exclude the supernatural. Spencer decides that the world is appearance and our knowledge of it depends on human nature. So the question really arises as to the soul nature of the human being and the nature of the self-conscious ego.

A high point of idealistic thought is reached with the trio of German thinkers, Hegel, Fichte and Schelling.

They represent the view that creative thinking, i.e. thinking not tied to the sense world, is the key to the development of the ego which then experiences its unity with the spiritual world.

Whatever philosophical statements may have been expressed, or whatever philosophical systems may have been created by the above thinkers, one thing is obvious and that is that they are striving energetically to try to discover the nature of man and his relationship with the world. They seek in the self-conscious mind a source of knowledge which illuminates the world. The soul is surrounded by a world that reveals itself to the senses but it is also aware of its own inner creative life.

According to Emerson great men are incarnated when others have prepared the ground. Rudolf Steiner was born in 1861 and with a sense of mission he began his anthroposophical or spiritual-scientific work at about the turn of the century. Earlier he had published a work on Goethe, *Goethe's World Conception*, and *The Philosophy of Freedom*, translated into English also as *The Philosophy of Spiritual Activity*. These are relevant to our considerations in the next chapters. The subtitle of *The Philosophy of Spiritual Activity* is *A basis for a modern world conception*, and a note included on the title page of early editions states: 'The results of observing the human soul according to the methods of natural science'.

Thinking: The Gateway to Knowledge

In the Babylonian story of Gilgamesh is an episode that throws light on the reason for man's search for knowledge. Gilgamesh, the king, represents the forward evolutionary development of mankind and in the story he wishes to go on a journey, which we can interpret as something taking place in the soul world. But first he seeks guidance from the Sun-god who wants to know the reason for the journey. Gilgamesh explains that he is tired of the city; he wants to go where no man's name is written to set up a monument to the gods (i.e. he is tired of the physical and seeks the spiritual). Then he asks, 'Why did you give me the desire for this adventure if it is not to be fulfilled?' It is the cry of a man seeking to know his own nature and his own destiny.

For modern man, in the welter of civilization, the cry is even more urgent. He seeks facts; he seeks explanations. In this day and age man no longer wants to believe; he wants to know. He requires more of the world than the world immediately gives him. Whatever or whoever has placed him into the world has bestowed many gifts on him but also many desires. Among these is his thirst for knowledge.

The fact that man feels himself to be a part of nature and yet separated from it has already been mentioned. What is it that has been separated out? What is it within us that is akin to nature apart from the physical? The answer has already been indicated—the power of thought.

Every explanation begins with thought and thought is a spiritual activity. It is not an automatic process like digestion. Although thought may be activated in connection with objects, it also has another side. One can use thought, for instance, to create shapes in the mind that are independent of sense impressions. The mind can create in imagination. The materialist may say that the brain produces thoughts but matter cannot really engage in active thinking. It would be more correct to say that the brain provides the instrument for thought.

We come back to Goethe. For him there are no two worlds. There exists only an abounding nature who pours forth her spirit into the world both of nature and of man.

The following extracts illustrate his outlook. They are from his 'Essay on Nature', freely translated:

Nature! We are surrounded by her, entwined with her and unable to escape from her.

Unasked and unwarned, she takes us into the circle of her dance and carries us along until we are weary and fall from her arms.

She creates new forms, but the new are always the old.

She builds and destroys.

She lives in countless children but the mother, where is she?

She is the outstanding artist. Each one of her works is a separate creation, yet all are parts of the one.

All men are within her and she is in all.

Life is her fairest invention, death her means to create more life.

We obey her laws even when we resist them.

We work with her even when we would work against her.

She has no speech nor language but she creates tongues and hearts through which she feels and speaks.

She is totality. Everything exists in her always.

For Goethe it is the same spiritual force which works throughout created nature as works in man. His attitude is this: Here I am with my physical body. The world outside is made up of the same matter. Because of this relationship my physical eye perceives physical things. In the plant is a superphysical force but also the same force is in me and if I do not perceive the superphysical in the plant it is because my own faculties are not sufficiently developed.

Goethe had a universality of outlook. He sought the whole. He realized that the different manifestations in the plant world were parts of one whole and he set out to find the universal mother. What he found is of tremendous importance. He discovered the *Urpflanze*, the archetypal plant. This is the universal creative force that manifests in an individual way in each plant but it does not exist physically. It is a supersensible force that may be perceived if the human mind is sufficiently developed.

What then is Goethe's particular attitude to knowledge and the obtaining of knowledge?

For him, there is no such thing as an object and idea—the idea is expressed in the object. Whereas some philosophers see reality only in ideas and others in a world of perception free of ideas, Goethe unites object and idea.

Whereas Kant says man has nothing to do with the thing-in-itself, Goethe says the same principle works in both. Goethe's view is that the phenomena reveal themselves fully to a man who approaches them with a free, unbiased spirit of observation and with a developed inner life in which the ideas of things manifest themselves. The question might arise as to why people see differently and the answer he gives is that every person has his own truth but this is only a part of one whole.

Goethe realized that the spiritual force working in the phenomena revealed itself to him at the same time as he watched the material object or process. There is no 'behind the phenomena'. He sought to find the relationship between thinking about objects and the objects themselves.

To begin with, objects appear as single entities but the process of thinking creates interrelationships. Outside of myself are the objects; thinking is my own activity. Thinking discovers something other than what is given by the senses. It finds what is hidden from the senses. Sense perception provides one side of reality, thinking the other. The thought then that lives in the mind is what is contained in the object and as such it is objective. Knowledge is the product of the activity of the human mind, i.e. spiritual activity. Thoughts belong to the reality of the sensibly perceived. They manifest inwardly in man. Thought and sense-perception are a single essence.

If we think about the nature of thinking it is clear that thinking makes the rest of experience intelligible. But the nature of thinking is given to us by nature. 'The World thinks in me.' Knowledge is perception and thinking. This is the attitude that Goethe assumed. He applied his method to the study of plant and animal but stopped short of the human being.

One could sum up Goethe's achievements in this particular respect as follows:

1 He practises 'observe and think', not like his predecessors Bacon and Aristotle but in a quite new way which leads him to:
2 The epochal discovery of the plant archetype which in its nature participates in thought and being. This leads to:
3 The vital principle of metamorphosis in plant and animal life.

The roles of observation and thinking in order to acquire knowledge have already been discussed. The next step to attain further knowledge is to consider the activity of thinking itself.

One has to differentiate in the first place between ordinary everyday thinking and the active concentrated thinking that can be used as a means of cognition. In ordinary parlance we 'think' we will go for a walk; we 'think' to take a drink, have a sandwich. We 'think' something is good or bad, attractive or otherwise. This sort of thinking is something that happens, something that is usually sparked off by some subjective experience and that for the most part occurs unconsciously. This is not thinking in the search for knowledge.

When our thinking is directed to a particular object then our consciousness is directed towards this object. But the object need not necessarily be something belonging to the outer world. Object in this sense can be something within ourselves—our feeling, our will, the content of our ideas. Without our thinking objects would appear as pure percepts and there would be no cohesion. Thinking establishes a relationship. It is through thinking that man connects himself with the world but it is also through thinking that he becomes conscious of himself as something separate. It might be thought that thinking is subjective but it is only through thinking that the human being becomes aware of his own subjectivity. It must therefore have an objective quality. Thinking is therefore an organ of perception which enables us to correlate the information given by the physical organs through sense impressions.

There are two aspects of thinking:

The content of ideas

The necessary inner activity which brings the ideas to consciousness.

It is with the latter that we must now concern ourselves.

Thinking is an activity that arises within ourselves and it is
of our own making. Normally it does not come naturally to
think about thinking. While the presence of all other objects is
given, and we can direct our thinking to them, in the case of
thinking we ourselves create the object but observation of it
can normally only take place later. Even to do this requires
practice but a further development of thinking is also possible.

It is not unknown for a light to dawn in the soul which we
call intuition. It is often seemingly accidental but more likely it
follows after we have been pondering something over a period
of time. But it can come about through concentrated effort.
We think, and think, and suddenly we see the point. Some
revelation is vouchsafed us. This we can also call intuition.
The light or the intuition comes from somewhere and the place
it comes from is the spiritual world. The greater the capacity of
the mind, the easier will be the attainment of the intuition. We
can equate intuition in this sense with a manifestation of a
spiritual reality.

By a process of training that also includes moral development, i.e. the ability to cast aside subjective elements, intuition
can become perceptible. It becomes a spiritual experience.
Thinking in ordinary consciousness stands apart from perceiving, but higher thinking is itself a form of perception. It is
spiritual perception. Higher thinking and spiritual perception
are one.

We could approach this spiritual activity in another way.

When an object registers its existence in the mind we speak
of a percept. The percept is what is observed. By linking
percepts together in the process of thinking one arrives at the
concept. The concept is nothing material but it has existence.
Let us take the specific case of a plant. If I wish to know more
about a plant, I can weigh it, measure it, analyse it and find so
much potash, so much carbon, etc. But have I really got to
know the plant? I know something, but to know it wholly I
must know it in the entirety of its growth and development. A

plant is in a continual state of movement. First I might consider the seed, but the seed is not the plant. Placed in soil, there will appear in a few weeks shoot and leaves. Day by day there will be change. Eventually a blossom will appear which will fade and die, giving place to seed formation. Thus at every moment I look at a plant, I know that I am seeing only a part of it. To get a picture and an understanding of the whole plant I must visualize its whole growth and metamorphosis from seed to shoot, from shoot and leaves to flower, from flower to seed and this I can do by the mental process of thinking. Thus I gain a concept of the plant. But in the plant there must be some supersensible principle at work that parallels my concept. So the spiritual that lives in the plant is one with my thinking. Although the concept has arisen within me, it is not subjective. Other observers and thinkers would arrive at the same concept. Thus we are dealing with an objective reality. It is obvious that my sense impression of the plant has stimulated me to think, so that what I think must be connected with it. My concentration on the phenomena manifest to the senses will enable me to reach the reality expressed in it.

A Philistine might say that this is all fancy and that only the object is real, but then he is denying his own activity of thinking which makes him able to pass judgement. The object provides one side of knowledge.

The concept, then, is something that arises within me. It is a manifestation—albeit for the moment spiritual and non-perceptible—of something real, and the something real beyond the concept is a spiritual reality. In the case of the plant it is what Goethe calls the *Urpflanze*, the archetypal plant, i.e. that which as a spiritual force lives in all plants. If thinking is developed further, it becomes perception; we see our thoughts. We shall have penetrated to a sphere where our thoughts do not merely reproduce outer things but where they are experiences in themselves. That is to say that there is spiritual reality in living thought and spiritual realities are experienced in pure thinking. This is knowledge arising from thought but also transcending it. Thought becomes perceptible.

It must be repeated that this stage of thinking is only attained through training that includes not only the training of thinking but also of feeling and willing. This higher thinking can only be attained if all elements of subjectivity are negated. Ultimate truth can only be acquired when something is grasped that is not influenced by the senses.

By outer observation the thinking processes are strengthened. By inner activity the soul qualities are transformed. What lives in the purified thinking is the spiritual counterpart of what is observed. Thinking becomes spiritual vision.

Moral Implications

The use of the senses alone does not attain complete reality. Thinking leads to a knowledge of that which is beyond sense perception, to concepts, to spiritual reality.

In grasping concepts or perceiving the spiritual, thinking merges with the Divine Mind, the spiritual foundation of the world. If man can penetrate thus far, he can recognize universal truth and this is true for all men. Since truth is universal, the more people who can recognize it the more likely will be the establishment of the brotherhood of man.

Morality consists in expressing the ideal but requires action.

In the normal way action is motivated in a number of ways. It may be instinctive; it may be due to feeling, to impulse, to ideas (in the narrow sense). These are subjective, and if one follows their dictates it cannot be said that the deed is accomplished as a result of high ideals. But if a person can attain to truth and then direct his will to the action he is acting as a free being in carrying out what he recognizes as necessity. The will is activated not by the call of duty (Kant) but by the ideal.

In this connection we might quote Rudolf Steiner's contra-statement to Kant's call to Duty: 'Freedom, thou kindly and humane name, thou that dost comprise all that is morally most lovable, all that my manhood most prizes, and that makest me the servant of nobody, thou that settest up no mere law, but awaitest what my moral love itself will recognize as law because in the face of every merely imposed law it feels itself unfree.' (*The Philosophy of Spiritual Activity*, chapter 9.)

Thinking and the transformation of thinking into spiritual perception leads therefore not only to knowledge but to deeds in the service of mankind. For man personally not only is the thirst for knowledge assuaged but he finds satisfaction in fulfilling ideals that have become a part of his being.

4

THE MISSION OF CHRIST

Millions of people all over the world profess to a belief in
Christianity and its message of love and brotherhood yet there
is precious little evidence of it among the so-called Christian
nations. On the other hand there is much outward testimony
to its influence. The cathedrals, churches and chapels in the
villages, towns and cities of the Christian world illustrate this.
The Bible is the world's best selling book. In the western
world, time is reckoned from the birth of Christ; our main
festivals are connected with His life. Countless words have
been written and spoken on various aspects of Christianity.
Wars have been waged in support of it and as a result of
various interpretations. The life of Christ has been made the
subject of plays and films.

Is it not strange that Christianity has had such an impact on
the world when it cannot even be proved in the accepted sense
that Christ ever lived at all? The Gospels are records of a sort
but they are not reliable historical documents. They are a
mixture of apparent fact and symbolism and do not even agree
in content. Christ himself left no record in writing.

As soon as one begins to think about Christ and Christianity one runs into problems. Many explanations are offered
but often they seem trivial and superficial, and at times con-
tradictory. Who was the Christ? What is meant by Christ the
Saviour? What is the meaning of original sin, redemption,
resurrection? What is one to understand by life everlasting?

These matters have occupied great minds for centuries.
Since historical records are non-existent and might be difficult
to comprehend even if they did exist, the ordinary human
mind applies reasoning and speculation with results that may,

or may not, be correct. But there is a record of all Earth's events available to those who can decipher it. This is a sort of imprint in the spiritual world that can be read by one who has the faculty of penetrating beyond the physical. Such a person was Rudolf Steiner and what he has to say provides a coherent account and explanation of world evolution, including the events in Palestine. Nevertheless it is not easy to understand these matters, neither is it to be expected since the advent of Christ is acknowledged as the greatest event in human evolution.

The understanding of Christianity is central to Rudolf Steiner's work, however much it may appear otherwise. In his writings and lecture courses the subject is dealt with extensively and further references to Christ and the Christ impulse are scattered throughout his works. He gave a series of lectures on each of the different Gospels and on the Apocalypse. These are not commentaries as such but elucidation of his world outlook in connection with Christianity. To study all that he has said in this connection might prove the study of a lifetime and it must therefore be appreciated that what follows here can only be considered bare outlines of the main themes.

A central thought to hold in mind is that Christ was a sublime cosmic Being who descended to the Earth and incarnated as man in order to bring new, revitalizing forces into the Earth's spiritual atmosphere. Through this deed man is enabled to shake off the fetters of materialism into which he had been seduced at the Fall. It is not what Christ taught that is of paramount importance but what He was, and what He gave. Christ infused the Earth aura with His being and in so doing gave man the ability to acquire new forces. Thus Christianity is not a sectarian or national religion. Christ came for all men. His advent was a decisive turning point in world history.

In the process of evolution the mind of man changes. What may be right at one time is not necessarily so at another. Many people no longer look to the church as the intermediary between themselves and God (the spiritual world) but seek a personal relationship. This is in keeping with the newly developed ego-consciousness. *Belief* is no longer sufficient; the modern mind requires *knowledge*. An understanding of the Christ event from the modern standpoint is essential. This shows that through the power of Christ direct knowledge of the spiritual world or, in biblical terms, the Kingdom of God, can be attained. Such knowledge is more than ever necessary in the present chaotic state of the world. Man needs to be reassured concerning his spiritual origin and nature and of his immortality.

Much of the following may appear strange at first sight. It is a summary of events as described by Rudolf Steiner, taken from his reading of the cosmic script. It must also be said that matters are much more complex than would appear from the reading of this chapter and only intense study of Dr Steiner's own works can yield a more perfect understanding.

Man's Expulsion from Paradise

In the Bible we read the story of the expulsion of Adam and Eve from the Garden of Eden. It is symbolic of the descent of man from the spiritual world to the physical. Formerly he had existed as a purely spiritual being, but now he has acquired a physical counterpart. This descent to the material world was due to the activity of the so-called Spirits of Adversity (Lucifer or the devil) who 'tempted' man. They 'opened his eyes' and awakened passions and desires which affected the physical body so that it lost its original purity.

The time of these events lies a long way back. In vol. 2, p. 12, of this work the various Post-Atlantean epochs of civilization have been described, namely: Ancient India, Ancient Persia, Egypt/Chaldea, Greece/Rome and the present. Before these was the age of Atlantis and, before that, of Lemuria. The continent of Atlantis was situated in the region of the present Atlantic ocean, i.e. between Europe/Africa and the Americas. Lemuria was in the area of the present Indian ocean. These continents have now, for the most part, disappeared. The story of Noah and the flood refers to the sinking of Atlantis.

The so-called Fall took place in the Lemurian period. At that time the Earth was in a much more mobile and liquid state. At the beginning of the period the human spirit did not inhabit a physical body. A change came about through the Spirits of Adversity. Lucifer tempted man. He told him that he could become like God, knowing good and evil. He instilled into man an enhanced sense of self, giving him thereby the prospect of freedom. But with freedom comes the possibility of choice, good or evil. The soul nature of man was contaminated and desire opened his eyes to the material world, i.e. he took on a physical form. His consciousness changed and he came to know sickness and death.

The descent into matter and the preoccupation with it was not a single event. In Atlantis, other Spirits of Adversity (known as Ahrimanic), sought to beguile man into believing that the material world was the only reality. Such temptations continued and have persisted to the present day, but since the incarnation of Christ and the availability of the forces that he brought with Him man has the ability to redeem the evil influences.

Such redemption, however, does not happen overnight. Just as remnants of spiritual vision linger on, so does the effect of the Fall, and counteraction becomes possible in accordance with historical developments.

New faculties within man began to develop at the time of the Reformation and Renaissance. In the course of time new powers from the spiritual world are made accessible to man. If he chooses to avail himself of them, personal spiritual effort and exertion are required.

Furthermore, spiritual science speaks of various ages in the history of mankind. One of these is known as Kali Yuga (the Dark Age) which ended in 1899. At this time the spiritual atmosphere—so to speak—brightened. The spiritual world came nearer.

The new possibilities for spiritual perception are connected with the development of the ego.

The Development of Ego-consciousness

The fact that people of the past were not conscious of themselves as individualities is evidenced by history. People were
led by divinely inspired leaders and felt themselves essentially
as members of a tribe or family, behaving in unison as a
corporate body. At the same time they enjoyed a measure of
spiritual vision. They were directly aware of the existence of a
spiritual world in which lived human souls and beings of other
orders.

In Egyptian times, about 2000 BC, the awareness of the
spiritual world was already fading and hence began the preoccupation with the significance of death. In Greek times the
faculty of spiritual perception became even dimmer and the
power of thinking developed in its place. (See vol. 1, chapter 3
of this work.) At this period it was said, 'Better a beggar on
Earth than a king in the realm of the shades'. It is significant
also that only in the Greek epoch does a feeling of conscience
develop. Before that man had experienced apparitions known
as the Eumenides, or the Furies, which were creations of his
own wrongdoing. Now conscience became an inner force.

With the loss of spiritual vision, i.e. direct divine guidance,
there came a feeling of increasing independence, a feeling of
individuality.

It was the Luciferic forces that put man on the downward
path but it was also the Luciferic forces that gave man his first
feeling of self. However, he did not become fully self-conscious
immediately at the time of the Fall. We may compare the
development with human growth. The child has an ego but in
the earliest years it has no capacity of self-direction. When it
begins to say 'I' at about the age of three, it is beginning to
differentiate between itself and the rest of the world but still
not really consciously. Only in adulthood is full awareness of
'I am an I' experienced. Humanity follows the same pattern.

Similarly, consciousness of the ego has only developed in
the course of time. Historically, we can say that a certain peak
is reached with the advent of Rome when the law is established
as between man and man. But the birth of Christ took place in
Roman times and therefore we can equally well say that man

becomes conscious of his ego at the time of Christ. It was, in fact, the advent of Christ that gave man this possibility.

The development of ego-consciousness becomes more obvious with the Reformation and the Renaissance. It is evidenced by the activities of a whole host of independent thinkers in realms of science and the fact that portraits (individualities) are painted by the great painters. In due course freedom from domination of every kind becomes a goal. The French and American revolutions are symptomatic of this striving. Even the industrial revolution can be considered in this light as it held the promise of freedom from toil. The great philosophers strive for freedom in the realm of thought and seek to learn the nature of the self. In our own times ego-consciousness reaches another peak.

But ego-consciousness has a direct relationship with the material world. Contact with the physical brings about an awakening. Running into an object makes us very conscious of it. Thus contact with material things brings about a feeling of self, of individuality, of ego. 'The object is something outside of myself and I therefore differentiate' is the experience. However, if the process goes too far and only the material aspect is considered without the spiritual, the soul withers. A parched soul affects the body. Historically, the physical condition of human bodies was deteriorating before the advent of Christ, making it difficult for human spirits to incarnate in them.

At this point Christ incarnated and brought a new revitalizing force to the Earth. Man had lost the connection with the divine but the divinity came to man. The quality with which he impregnated the spiritual atmosphere of the Earth is a force by which the ego, by its own efforts, can re-open the spiritual gates. 'I am the Light of the World' means 'I am the first to give expression to the "I am" and the impulse for it'.

The Cosmic Christ and His Descent to Earth

The Gospel of St John begins with the words 'In the beginning was the Word and the Word was with God and the Word was

God ... and the Word became flesh and dwelt among us.' St John is referring to a creative force or Being, a cosmic spirit or a principle that has been connected with mankind since time began and which eventually appeared on the Earth clothed in physical form.

It would be natural therefore to try to trace some historical sequence.

Religion means the establishment of a connection with the divine. Different peoples have sought this connection in different ways according to their state of mind. It must be appreciated that this has changed in the course of evolution. In former times men perceived creative beings or their creative life-power; they perceived their God or gods in different spheres. We can observe this if we study the religious outlook in the various pre-Christian epochs of the Post-Atlantean age. In fact religion is a characteristic of this period. In earlier times man's mind was more attuned to the spiritual than to the physical, and since there was direct connection with the divine there was no need to establish it.

Before the continent of Atlantis finally disappeared, the initiate (Noah) led a selected group to central Asia from whence a new impulse radiated.

The wise men of Ancient India (*c*. 9000 BC looked up to a universal divine power which they called Brahma and whose home was the spiritual sphere of the Sun. What lived in man was also Brahma, an extract of the divine substance. As the Sun pours its light and strength physically through the universe so was there also an outpouring of spiritual power. This power was called Vishva Karman, a name that means the Word.

In Ancient Persia the great Zarathustra spoke with the Radiant Star, Ahura Mazdao, the cosmic spirit who lived in the aura of the Sun. Light and darkness were entities. On the instructions of Ahura Mazdao men cultivated the earth to bring light into darkness. They spoke truth to bring light into darkness in the moral sphere.

The Egyptians had a Sun-god, Ra. The one who represented the Sun forces as far as Earth was concerned, which man also carried within him, was the god-king, Osiris. The Egyptians

perceived forces coming to the Earth from the Sun and also
from the Moon, which reflects the light of the Sun. Akhena-
ton, who ascended the Egyptian throne in 1375 BC, declared
that the great Being whose home had been in the Sun was no
longer there.

In Greece men did not have the same feeling for the one Sun
spirit as did the Persians. They had a dual concept. On the one
hand they looked to the physical Sun, which they termed
'Helios', but they also felt the presence of a spiritual Sun that
permeates both Earth and man. The spiritual atmosphere they
called Zeus. His son, Phoebus Apollo, was the most widely
revered and influential of the Greek gods. His functions were
many. Among them was the duty of communicating the will of
his father to men. He was the protector of crops and herds.
'Phoebus' means 'bright' or 'pure' and Phoebus Apollo was
looked upon as a Sun-god. He personifies the spiritual Sun-
forces which the Greeks felt to be active in the elements and in
nature.

Contemporary with the Egyptians and the Greeks were the
Jews, the 'chosen' people, directed by their personal god
Jehovah. For reasons connected with evolution and beyond
our immediate consideration, Jehovah had made his spiritual
home in the Moon-sphere, and just as the Moon reflects the
sunlight so Jehovah reflected the Sun-spirit. In very mundane
terms he was the acting representative.

(It is interesting to note that the Jews had originated from
Ur, 'Ur of the Chaldees', a city that was a centre of Moon
worship, and that other peoples of the period also worshipped
the Moon.)

In the course of time the divinity came nearer to the Earth
and Moses experienced the god in the elements, as 'a pillar of
cloud by day and a pillar of fire by night'. He heard a voice in
the burning bush announcing itself as the 'I am'.

Mithras, originally a Persian god and popular with the
Roman legions, was a Sun-god. Druid worship, too, was
connected with the Sun.

In all these instances we have to appreciate a connection
with the Sun, and in the sequence of the epochs of civilization
we can observe how men experienced the spirit of the Sun

approaching the Earth. Vishva Karman, Ahura Mazdao, Osiris, Apollo are all identified with the spiritual essence of the Sun. This essence or being seems to be far away in Indian times but comes nearer to the Earth in the course of time. Just before the birth of Christ it is in the immediate neighbourhood; then it is clothed with a human form.

This was something unprecedented in history. In earlier times men may have been guided or inspired by gods, or even have perceived them, but now a divine Being actually became man. It was a new experience in the cosmic order.

Let us quote St Augustine: 'That which is now called the Christian religion existed already among the ancients, even in the earliest days of the human race. When Christ appeared in the flesh, the true religion, which was already in existence, was called Christianity.'

We also have the words of St John Crysostom (golden-mouthed), the greatest orator of the early Christian church: 'The Kingdom of heaven has come down ... we have seen the Sun wandering on the Earth.'

The Incarnation

For such a Being as the Christ to incarnate, very special preparation was necessary.

This particular phase of the story begins with Abraham, who was called upon by the Lord to be the father of a great nation. The Lord in this case is Jehovah. Under his guidance and that of later inspired human leaders the Jewish race grew and developed. Strict laws of conduct were imposed. No intermarriage with other races was allowed and a particular type of human being evolved. The mission of the Jewish people was to provide a suitable physical vehicle for the Christ spirit to enter.

It is difficult to reconcile the two Gospel accounts of the birth of Jesus with one another but they become clear when it is recognized that they refer to different children.

St Matthew describes a boy called Jesus who was born in

Bethlehem of the Solomon line of David. St Luke writes about
a boy, also called Jesus, who was born in Bethlehem and who
was a descendant of the Nathan line. In the St Matthew child
the mighty individuality of Zarathustra was incarnated. In the
other Jesus lived an entity—a provisional ego one could say—
which had never before appeared on the Earth. If one thinks of
the ego as a drop of the Divine Essence, then this was an
original, an innocent ego in the sense that having had no
earthly experience it had acquired no karma and had remained
uninfluenced by all the events of earthly evolution.

(In passing, it is interesting to note that certain painters of
the Renaissance depict the Madonna with two children.)

The sequence of events is this—two of David's sons were
Solomon the King and Nathan the Priest, and in the course of
generations there were contemporary descendants of each
called Joseph and each had a wife called Mary. The St Matthew pair had their home in Bethlehem, took refuge in Egypt
to avoid the massacre and then came to live in Nazareth.
Other children were born to them.

The Joseph and Mary of St Luke lived in Nazareth but their
boy was born in Bethlehem as related in the Gospel story.
They returned to Nazareth and lived in close proximity to the
other family but there were no more children of this union.
They had not been involved in the massacre of the innocents as
their child was born subsequent to this event.

The two children were very different in disposition. The
Solomon Jesus was clever in a worldly sense, endowed with
great intelligence and talent; the Nathan boy was untalented in
the intellectual sense but blessed with an unusual kindness of
heart and a special gift of radiating love. When the children
were 12 years of age, there occurred that dramatic event which
is known as the scene in the temple. The parents of the Nathan
child had journeyed with others to Jerusalem but missed him
on the way back. On searching they found him in the temple
disputing with the learned doctors. On reprimanding him for
causing them distress they were told that he had to be about
his Father's business. These events and remarks were something which greatly puzzled them and which they could not
understand, although his mother may have had an inkling

since we read in St Luke that she kept all these sayings in her heart. Then we are told that Jesus 'increased in wisdom and stature, and in favour with God and man'.

A dramatic event had taken place which ordinary mortals may find a little difficult to comprehend.

The Zarathustra individuality who had lived in the body of the Solomon Jesus transferred the scene of his activity to the Nathan boy and became, so to speak, the ego of this person. The new ego then worked within this physical frame to the thirtieth year to make it capable of receiving the Being of the Christ. The relinquished body of the Solomon Jesus died soon afterwards and so did the mother of the Nathan child. The father of the Solomon child also died and the widowed father of the Nathan child took the widow with her children into his home. From this time onward then we are concerned with only one Jesus boy, one who combined earthly wisdom with heavenly love.

This Jesus followed his father's trade of carpenter. He became a travelling craftsman, a journeyman. Finding favour with God and man indicates that he was welcome wherever he went. He showed particular interest in the religious situation and he was connected with the religious community known as the Essenes. He was not, however, happy in their presence. They lived in settlements, withdrawn from the mass of the people. They considered the Pharisees and Sadducees to be self-righteous and hypocritical. Orthodox Judaism they thought degenerate and believed themselves to be the genuine upholders of the faith. Although they possessed great spirituality, Jesus found them too self-centred, and preferred to live among the common folk and share the common lot.

When Jesus was 30 the baptism in the Jordan took place. It was another great transformation. This was the moment when the actual Christ-spirit supplanted the previous individuality and became the new ego. From this time onward to the crucifixion we can speak of a God incarnate, a God in a human frame, Christ in Jesus—Jesus Christ.

The Turning Point of Time

The fact has already been mentioned that, in the course of his evolution, the human being became free from divine guidance and conscious of his ego. To find his way back to the spiritual, consciously, through the ego, a Divine Being came to the physical plane to point the way.

Through the example of His life Christ demonstrated and taught the existence of a spiritual world and the way to attain it. He came to give men the possibility of regaining consciously what had been lost and to inspire them to this end. His deed is the antidote to that of Lucifer. He gives a glimpse into future evolution.

Let us consider three aspects of the Christ impulse:

1 The example of His life
2 His teaching
3 The cosmic power.

To understand what is implied here it is necessary to look back into the pre-Christian 'Mysteries'. For those not familiar with this term, let it not be confused with the usual meaning of the word 'mystery'.

At all times in history there have been those who by special gift or special development have had access to the spiritual world. They are known as 'initiates'. In cases where the mass of people had spiritual vision, the initiates were those who had enhanced faculties. These individuals participated in the 'Mysteries', i.e. they communed with the gods. By the time of Christ this faculty had almost died out and the Mysteries had fallen into decadence. Had there been no new impulse men would have sunk too deeply into matter and have lost touch with the spiritual worlds entirely.

The decadence of the Mysteries is directly connected with the descent of Christ to the Earth. One of the things that the initiates of old had experienced was the divine foundation of the world, the One who was in the beginning, i.e. the Christ, although the term was not used. But now the One had left the cosmic heights and was on the Earth.

It is thus that we may understand the proclamation of John

the Baptist 'Repent, for the kingdom of heaven is at hand', i.e. Change your attitude, change your way of thinking, the Divine Being is no longer to be found in cosmic heights but here on Earth.

The spiritual vision had faded and man was very engrossed with the material world, hence what was demonstrated in the physical could be understood. Thus men observed the life and deeds of Christ on the physical plane and Christ himself demonstrates openly and publicly what had formerly only been attainable through the Mysteries. His teaching showed the way of spiritual development and the way to attain spiritual perception. His deed brought rejuvenating forces from the cosmos into the Earth.

The example of His life

Christ was a leader who had not undergone the acknowledged training in the Mysteries and this was one reason why there was such opposition to him from the Jewish sects in Palestine.

One striking demonstration that He gave, showing that the old order was changed, was in the raising of Lazarus. This was an old type initiation brought about by the Christ publicly and not in the secrecy of the Mystery temple.

The Gospel accounts seem to describe very strange events if they are taken at their face value. They can only be understood if we appreciate that some of them are symbolic. For instance, reference is often made to going up into the mountain or being by the sea. These can be understood as portraying different levels of consciousness. That is to say, Christ is speaking in the spirit or is communing with His disciples in a spiritual state. The spiritual world is portrayed as physical.

Another matter was His gift of healing. In His time the human constitution was different from what it is today and healing by the laying-on of hands was not unusual. The physicians of that time were trained in the Mystery schools and it was possible for them to direct the flow of divine forces to a sick person. What was remarkable in Christ is that He could do it without training, but it is to be noted that the sick had to participate in the healing process. 'Thy faith hath made thee whole.'

But Christ's life itself parallels the initiation process. In the Mysteries the neophyte (novice or candidate) had to follow a strict code of conduct. He had to resist temptations both of the physical world and of self-aggrandisement.

In the case of Christ we are told that after the baptism He went into the wilderness. Is this real, symbolic, or both? A feeling of loneliness, of being cut off, of being thrown onto one's own resources, is a common fate of man. Christ experienced this and then came what is described as the Temptation—to turn stones to bread, to cast Himself down from the temple, to bow down and worship the tempter. Christ does not seek power in this way. He resisted the temptation through the power of His own Being, what in man we should term the 'I' or the ego.

An interesting sidelight is provided by St Mark who tells us that Christ was then among the wild beasts, and Angels ministered unto him. We are given the picture of the human being, of human nature, between beast and Angel.

To become an initiate in the old Mystery schools, the candidate had to develop particular qualities. He had to develop an attitude of gratitude to all that is of a lower order, to learn to accept rebuffs without retaliation, to renounce blood ties, to endure suffering, to experience evil and the equivalent of death in order to be reawakened in the spirit. All these are illustrated in the life experiences of the Christ—the positive attitude, the rejection, the agony in the garden, the scourging, the crown of thorns, crucifixion, death and resurrection. In this case the events led to an actual death. Throughout all these experiences is the assertion of that power, the ego, which gives the possibility of saying 'I am'. Christ demonstrates not only the existence of the spirit but also its triumph.

The initiation process is also the way of development of the human being. By overcoming selfish passions and desires, by enduring and by positive activity man purifies his soul. Christ not only illustrated this but he also demonstrated developments which will take place in the far distant future.

To understand this we must recall the fourfoldness of the being of man, as described in vol. 1, chapter 1 of this work. Besides ego and astral body, man has an etheric and a physical. At the present stage of evolution man is able to take himself sufficiently in hand that he can begin to transform his astral body, i.e. to purify his soul. In time there will come a stage in human affairs when the etheric body also will be purified and transformed, and then the physical.

One who has spiritual vision would see the transformed etheric body as if radiating and this was the experience of the disciples at the event known as the Transfiguration.

With regard to the physical body, it will be remembered that in the story of the resurrection Christ appeared in a spiritual form—but there was a sequel. When the tomb was opened after three days, the physical body of Christ had gone. The explanation is that this physical body had been so permeated by the great cosmic spirit that its substance had dematerialized quickly. What the disciples saw was the purified physical form, i.e. the purified body permeated by the Christ forces. It was the body released from the forces of materialism, the non-physical, original pattern of a human body as it had first existed as a thought of the gods before it was clothed with the garment of flesh, but with this difference: it had been through the earthly process and was therefore an advance on the original creation of the Hierarchies. This is what can be understood as the resurrection of the body. In the course of evolution the physical body will be purged or transformed. The effects of the Fall will be cancelled and man will have advanced to a higher stage.

What was experienced and what existed in one personality on Earth for three years, humanity will develop in its evolution.

His teaching

Christ's teaching is also the way of initiation. What is His essential message? It might be epitomized in two sentences:

Seek ye first the Kingdom of God.
Love the Lord thy God and thy neighbour as thyself.

In modern terminology we call the Kingdom of God the spiritual world. The path to it is by purification of the soul and meditation (prayer), i.e. by inner activity. The development of morality is a necessity but times have changed since Moses proclaimed the Ten Commandments. These were given by the Sun-spirit speaking through Jehovah. Their purpose was to develop morality at a time when humanity did not possess the ability for giving itself direction from within.

In the Christ-like way of life the external law (the Ten Commandments) is no longer necessary since love and moral principles become part of human nature.

The Gospels are not primarily factual records. They were written by initiates from spiritual inspiration. They are to be understood as a path of development. The events described are part historic, part inner experience, part symbolic, or even all three combined. Nevertheless the Gospels contain what we might term the teaching of Christ and it is put very lucidly in the Sermon on the Mount.

An inner purification is required, a social awareness and responsibility, an enhanced mental alertness which will lead to the Kingdom of God—in other words, spiritual perception. Faith is also required but faith in the Gospel sense is not blind belief. When it is stated 'Thy faith hath made thee whole', it is implied that some active force has been set to work within the human being whereby spiritual sources are tapped sufficient to overcome the disability.

With spiritual perception man is conscious of the spiritual world and of himself as a spiritual being. Thus he may be aware of a transition but not of death. He is conscious of his immortality.

The cosmic power

We said already that the great cosmic spirit whom we call the Christ brought a new revitalizing spiritual substance to the Earth which now permeates our spiritual atmosphere in the same way that the air permeates the physical.

This must be understood in a literal sense but it may help

our understanding if we recall the fact that every human being affects the world in some way and also leaves an influence which continues after his death. How much greater then are the results of a Divine Being who has lived on Earth! Christ also experienced earthly death and in so doing united himself with earthly evolution. Whatever example he may have set, whatever ethical instruction he may have given, the important fact is that he brought with him a spiritual force which has been bestowed on the Earth to awaken the ego and the power of love. As a dissolving crystal will colour a whole volume of water, so has the Christ force permeated the spiritual atmosphere of the Earth. It means that there are now forces available to the human being which were not there before. It means that humanity now has new possibilities of advancing.

When Christ lived in the flesh, a cosmic power flowed from Him which gave Him the ability to heal. It stimulated the forces of the sick. After his death the Earth itself received this power. It gives man the possibility of transforming himself through his own will, of meeting evil and of overcoming it. It is there for every man or woman, of every race, of every nation.

The advent of Christ on Earth was a turning point in history but man has to work out his own salvation. In the ancient Mysteries the would-be initiate spent three days in a state of deathlike trance supervised and guided by priests. This is no longer the path of initiation for modern ego-conscious man. It was no longer the right path of initiation in Christ's day, since when mankind has evolved even further. During this period man has had the opportunity to savour the full flavour of materialism and, together with it, the consciousness of self. Man now has the forces within, given by Christ, to strive to a new understanding of things spiritual and to a new kind of perception. Evolution is continuous. To accept Christ as example or teacher is not sufficient. It is now a question of transforming oneself so that some positive force flows in from the spiritual world and then one may speak of Christ within or of the Higher Self. That is what it means to be a Christian.

To quote Rudolf Steiner: 'Christianity teaches the seeker to behold the Christ, to fill himself with the power of His image, to seek to become like Him and to follow after Him. Then his liberated ego needs no other law. Christ brings freedom from the law; then good will be done because of indwelling love within the soul.'

The Second Coming

According to modern scholars of the Greek language this popular phrase is a misnomer. The original Greek speaks not of a 'coming' but of a 'presence' or an 'appearance'. Had one of these words been used in the early translations, it is possible that a different understanding of the event would have been the result.

Whatever the expression, however, it must be realized that Christ's coming to Earth was a unique occasion which will not be repeated. Christ came to the Earth and he has remained united with it. His being is now to be found in the etheric substance of the Earth, in the spiritual atmosphere. In the Bible it is expressed that the coming (presence) will be 'in the clouds', 'to meet the Lord in the air'.

This event has to be understood not as a coming again of the Christ but as a raising of the human power to perceive Him spiritually. As men develop powers of spiritual perception, they will have an experience similar to that of Saul (St Paul) at Damascus. But there will be a difference. To St Paul it came as a shock but thanks to spiritual science mankind today has some knowledge of what to expect. Furthermore, it is not likely to be a sudden experience since the acquisition of spiritual vision is a gradual process. When a man eventually perceives Christ in the etheric, it will be an experience of blessedness and illumination.

READING LIST

Unless otherwise indicated, all books are published by Rudolf Steiner Press, England, or Anthroposophic Press, New York.

Works by Rudolf Steiner

Fundamental reading:

Occult Science—An Outline.

Theosophy (This title is to be understood in the original meaning of 'Divine Wisdom'.)

Knowledge of the Higher Worlds. How is it Achieved?

The Philosophy of Freedom. An alternative translation is entitled *The Philosophy of Spiritual Activity.*

As a general introduction to Anthroposophy:

At the Gates of Spiritual Science.

More advanced:

Rosicrucian Esotericism.

Theosophy of the Rosicrucian.

Reading for Chapter 1

Life between Death and Rebirth

Between Death and Rebirth

Reading for Chapter 2

The Spiritual Hierarchies

The Spiritual Guidance of Mankind

Reading for Chapter 3

The Philosophy of Freedom (or *The Philosophy of Spiritual Activity*)

The Riddles of Philosophy

Goethe's Conception of the World

Reading for Chapter 4

Christianity as Mystical Fact

From Jesus to Christ

The Spiritual Guidance of Mankind

The Christ Impulse and the Development of Ego-Consciousness

The True Nature of the Second Coming

By Alfred Heidenreich:

The Unknown in the Gospels (Floris Books, Edinburgh)

RUDOLF STEINER

aspects of his spiritual world-view

Anthroposophy

volume 1

Roy Wilkinson

Rudolf Steiner – herald of a new age
Reincarnation and karma
The spiritual nature of the human being
The development of human consciousness

96pp; 21.5 x 13.5 cm; illus; paperback; £5.95; ISBN 0 904693 47 3

TEMPLE LODGE PUBLISHING

RUDOLF STEINER

aspects of his spiritual world-view

Anthroposophy

volume 2

Roy Wilkinson

Evolution of the world and humanity
Relationships between the living and the dead
Forces of evil
The modern path of initiation

96pp; 21.5 × 13.5 cm; illus; paperback; £5.95; ISBN 0 904693 51 1

TEMPLE LODGE PUBLISHING